STAAR Grade 3 Mathematics Assessment Secrets

Study Guide

Your Key to Exam Success

STAAR Test Review for the
State of Texas Assessments of Academic Readiness

Dear Future Exam Success Story:

Congratulations on your purchase of our study guide. Our goal in writing our study guide was to cover the content on the test, as well as provide insight into typical test taking mistakes and how to overcome them.

Standardized tests are a key component of being successful, which only increases the importance of doing well in the high-pressure high-stakes environment of test day. How well you do on this test will have a significant impact on your future- and we have the research and practical advice to help you execute on test day.

The product you're reading now is designed to exploit weaknesses in the test itself, and help you avoid the most common errors test takers frequently make.

How to use this study guide

We don't want to waste your time. Our study guide is fast-paced and fluff-free. We suggest going through it a number of times, as repetition is an important part of learning new information and concepts.

First, read through the study guide completely to get a feel for the content and organization. Read the general success strategies first, and then proceed to the content sections. Each tip has been carefully selected for its effectiveness.

Second, read through the study guide again, and take notes in the margins and highlight those sections where you may have a particular weakness.

Finally, bring the manual with you on test day and study it before the exam begins.

Your success is our success

We would be delighted to hear about your success. Send us an email and tell us your story. Thanks for your business and we wish you continued success-

Sincerely,

Mometrix Test Preparation Team

TABLE OF CONTENTS

Top 15 Test Taking Tips

1. Know the test directions, duration, topics, question types, how many questions
2. Setup a flexible study schedule at least 3-4 weeks before test day
3. Study during the time of day you are most alert, relaxed, and stress free
4. Maximize your learning style; visual learner use visual study aids, auditory learner use auditory study aids
5. Focus on your weakest knowledge base
6. Find a study partner to review with and help clarify questions
7. Practice, practice, practice
8. Get a good night's sleep; don't try to cram the night before the test
9. Eat a well balanced meal
10. Wear comfortable, loose fitting, layered clothing; prepare for it to be either cold or hot during the test
11. Eliminate the obviously wrong answer choices, then guess the first remaining choice
12. Pace yourself; don't rush, but keep working and move on if you get stuck
13. Maintain a positive attitude even if the test is going poorly
14. Keep your first answer unless you are positive it is wrong
15. Check your work, don't make a careless mistake

Mathematics Assessment

Numbers, Operations, and Quantitative Reasoning

Number order and written numbers

Write each list of numbers from least to greatest, and write each number in words.
   a) 4,002; 280; 108,511; 9
   b) 75,600; 800,330; 300,001

   a) 9: nine; 280: two hundred eighty; 4,002: four thousand two; 108,511: one hundred eight thousand five hundred eleven
   b) 75,600: seventy five thousand six hundred; 300,001: three hundred thousand and one; 800,330: eight hundred thousand three hundred thirty

Place value

Write the place value of each digit in the following number: 14,059

   1: ten thousands
   4: thousands
   0: hundreds
   5: tens
   9: ones

Value of coins and bills

Example 1
Allison has one $1-dollar bill, two quarters, and 4 dimes in her bank. Find the total amount of money in Allison's bank.

It may help to draw a picture. Write the value of each bill or coin in its picture. Then add up the bills and coins to find the total money.

$1 + 0.25 + 0.25 + 0.10 + 0.10 + 0.10 + 0.10 = 1.90$
There is $1.90 in Allison's bank.

Example 2

Drew has two $20-dollar bills, one $5-bill, three nickels, and seven pennies. Determine the total amount of money Drew has.

It may help to draw a picture. Write the value of each bill or coin in its picture. Then add up the bills and coins to find the total money.

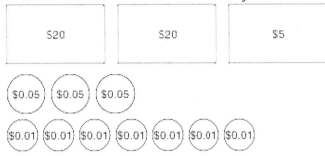

20 + 20 + 5 + 0.05 + 0.05 + 0.05 + 0.01 + 0.01 + 0.01 + 0.01 + 0.01 + 0.01 + 0.01 = 45.22
Drew has a total of $45.22.

Fraction names and symbols

Fractions are parts of whole numbers and are made up of one number (called the numerator) written above another number (called the denominator), with a sideways line between them. They are also named based on these numbers. If the fraction is three over eight, then it is called three eighths, and it is written, $\frac{3}{8}$.

Example

Name each fraction and write its symbol.

 a. Two over five
 b. One over three
 c. Four over eleven

 a. two fifths, $\frac{2}{5}$
 b. one third, $\frac{1}{3}$
 c. four elevenths, $\frac{4}{11}$

Models describing fractional parts

<u>Example 1</u>
Write a fraction, in numbers and words, to represent the shaded rectangles on the fraction strip below.

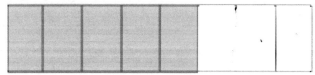

There are 8 total spaces of the fraction strip. This is the denominator of the fraction. There are 5 spaces that are shaded. This is the numerator. The fraction that represents the shaded spaces of the fraction strip is $\frac{5}{8}$. In words, this is five eighths.

<u>Example 2</u>
A cookie recipe asks for $1\frac{1}{2}$ sticks of butter. Draw the butter needed for the recipe.

Each stick of butter can be represented with a rectangle. Draw a rectangle to represent the first stick of butter. Since more than one whole stick is needed in the recipe, shade this entire stick to show that it is used in the recipe.

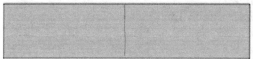

Draw a second rectangle to represent the additional butter needed in the recipe. The whole stick is not needed. Only the remaining butter, the $\frac{1}{2}$ stick, will be used. Divide the stick into two equal pieces, and shade one of the pieces to show the $\frac{1}{2}$ stick used in the recipe.

<u>Example 3</u>
Alex's mom brings $6\frac{3}{4}$ oranges to a soccer game. Draw the number of oranges she brought to the game.
The whole number is the number of whole oranges brought to the game. Each of these can be represented by a circle. Shade the entire circle to show the whole orange was used.

The fraction of an orange is only a portion of a circle. Divide a circle into three equal spaces, and shade two of them to represent the $\frac{3}{4}$ of an orange.

- 4 -

Addition and subtraction

Example 1
Chris brings $20 to the store. He spends $2 on a notebook. Determine how much money Chris has left after buying the notebook.

To find how much money Chris has left, subtract the cost of the notebook from the total amount of money Chris had before he bought the notebook.
Money before notebook − cost of notebook = money left
$20 − $2 = $18

Example 2
Lindsay and April both bring balloons to a birthday party. Lindsay brings 14 balloons, and April brings 8 balloons. Find the total number of balloons the girls brought to the party.

To find the total number of balloons, add together the balloons brought by each girl.
Lindsay's balloons + April's balloons = 14 + 8 = 22 balloons
The girls brought a total of 22 balloons to the party.

Example 3
Christian has $4, and Allison has $8. Determine how much money they have altogether.

To find out how much money Christian and Allison have altogether, add together the money that each person has. To help add the money, the dollars can be represented using circles. Draw circles to represent the dollars.
Christian:

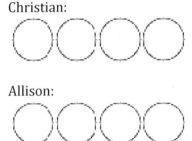

Allison:

To find the total money they have altogether, count the total dollars. There are 12. If each circle is worth $1, the total money that Christian and Allison have is $12.

Example 4
Austin has three cookies. He shares one cookie with Sarah. Describe how to find how many cookies he has left.

Austin starts with 3 cookies. He takes one of those cookies away, and gives it to Sarah. He now has one less cookie than he had before. To find the number of cookies that he has left, subtract 1 from 3: 3 − 1 = 2. He has 2 cookies left.

- 5 -

Multiplication

<u>Example 1</u>
Ms. Webber collects pictures from her students to create a yearbook. The yearbook is 15 pages long, and there are 4 pictures on each page. Find the total number of pictures in the yearbook.

To find the total number of pictures, multiply the number of pictures on each page by the number of pages. If there are 4 pictures on each page, and a total of 15 pages, then the total number of pictures in the yearbook is: $4 \cdot 15 = 60$. Addition can also be used to find the total number of pictures. If there are 15 pages, then add 4 fifteen times to find the total number of pictures on the 15 pages:
$4 + 4 + 4 + 4 + 4 + 4 + 4 + 4 + 4 + 4 + 4 + 4 + 4 + 4 + 4 = 60$ pictures

<u>Example 2</u>
Think of a problem that could be solved by finding the product: $4 \cdot 6$.

An example situation is: there are four students, and each student has six notebooks. Find the total number of notebooks. To find the total number of notebooks, multiply the number of students, 4, by the number of notebooks that each student has, 6: $4 \cdot 6 = 24$.

<u>Example 3</u>
Find the following products:
    1) $2 \cdot 6$
    2) $5 \cdot 3$
    3) $7 \cdot 9$
    4) $4 \cdot 11$
    5) $12 \cdot 10$

    1) $2 \cdot 6 = 12$
    2) $5 \cdot 3 = 15$
    3) $7 \cdot 9 = 63$
    4) $4 \cdot 11 = 44$
    5) $12 \cdot 10 = 120$

<u>Example 4</u>
A teacher estimates that it will take him 8 minutes to grade each student's test. He gave a test to 56 students. Determine how long it will take the teacher to grade all of the tests.

To find the total time, in minutes, that it will take the teacher to grade all of the tests, multiply the time it takes to grade each test by the number of students whose tests need to be graded. It takes 8 minutes to grade each test, and there are 56 students who took a test. The total time to grade all tests is: 8 minutes per test $\cdot$ 56 student tests = 448 minutes.

Division

Example 1
Mrs. Jan purchased pencils for her students. There are 10 students, and she purchased 40 pencils. If she wants to give each student the same number of pencils, find the number of pencils she should give to each student.

A diagram can be used to solve the problem. Mrs. Jan is dividing the total number of pencils, 40, by the total number of students, 10, to find the number of pencils for each student: 40 ÷ 10. Draw 40 pencils using line segments, then divide the pencils into groups of 10.

If 40 pencils are divided into groups of 10, there will be four total groups. Mrs. Jan should give each student 40 ÷ 10 = 4 pencils.

Example 2
T-shirts are sold in packages of multiple shirts. Four t-shirts are sold in one package for $8.00. Find the price of a single t-shirt.

To find the price of each t-shirt, divide the quantity of shirts in each package by the cost of the package.
$8.00 ÷ 4 = $2.00
The price per t-shirt is $2.00.

A picture can be drawn to find the total. Draw 8 squares to represent the 8 dollars, and divide them into 4 equal groups.

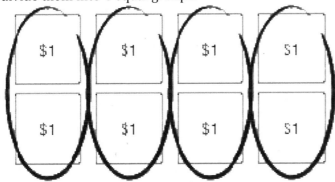

The size of each group is 8 ÷ 4.
8 ÷ 4 = 2.

Example 3
The fourth graders decide to hold a car wash to earn $810.00 for a class field trip. The students will earn $6.00 for each car that is washed. Find the number of cars that need to be washed to earn $810.00.

To find the number of cars the students need to wash, divide the total amount needed by the amount earned for each car that is washed. The students need to earn $810, and earn $6 for each car, so the total number of cars that need be washed is: $\frac{\$810}{\$6} = 135$. The total number of cars that need to be washed is 135.

- 7 -

Rounding to solve problems

Example 1
Mason needs 72 chocolate candies to give to 12 friends. The candies come in bags of 10. Determine how many bags of candy Mason needs to order.

Since the candies come in bags of 10, round the total number of candies needed up to the nearest 10; 72 rounded up to the nearest 10 is 80. The number of bags to order is the total candies ordered, 80, divided by the number of candies in each bag, 10: 80 ÷ 10 = 8. Mason needs to order 8 bags of candy.

Example 2
A store sells printer paper in packages of 100 sheets. Mrs. Fay is printing a test for her students. She needs 540 pieces of paper. Determine how many packages of paper she should buy.

Since the paper comes in packages of 100, round the total sheets needed up to the nearest 100; 540 rounded to the nearest 100 is 600. The number of packages to buy is the total pages, 600, divided by the number of sheets in each package, 100: 600 ÷ 100 = 6. Mrs. Fay needs to order 6 packages of paper.

Example 3
Mr. Watson buys two items from the store:
    1) pencils for $1.98
    2) a notebook for $0.85

Estimate to find the total cost of the two items.

First, round the cost of each item to the closest dollar. The pencils are $1.98, so the closest dollar is $2. The notebook is $0.85, so the closest dollar is $1. Next, add the rounded cost of each item to estimate the total cost:
$2 + $1 = $3
The estimated total cost is $3.

Example 4
Avery has $15. She buys a t-shirt that costs $8.25. Estimate how much money Avery has left after buying the t-shirt.

First, round the cost of the t-shirt to the nearest dollar. The t-shirt costs $8.25, so the closest dollar is $8. Next, subtract the rounded cost of the shirt from the amount of money Avery had before buying the shirt: $15 – $8 = $7.
Avery has approximately $7 left after buying the t-shirt.

Patterns, Relationships, and Algebraic Reasoning

Patterns

Example 1
Find the next number in each pattern:

    1) 2, 4, 6, 8, …
    2) 5, 10, 15, 20, …
    3) 60, 50, 40, 30, …

    1) The numbers are increasing by 2. Add 2 to the last number to find the next number: 2, 4, 6, 8, 8 + 2 = 10.
    2) The numbers are increasing by 5. Add 5 to the last number to find the next number: 5, 10, 15, 20, 20 + 5 = 25.
    3) The numbers are decreasing by 10. Subtract 10 from the last number to find the next number: 60, 50, 40, 30, 30 – 10 = 20.

Example 2
Draw the next figure in this pattern:

Look at the sides of each figure.
Figure 1: 3 sides
Figure 2: 4 sides
Figure 2: 5 sides

The number of sides on each figure is increasing by 1. The next figure will have 6 sides.

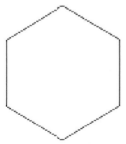

Example 3
Find the next figure in the pattern.

The first figure has 1 dot. The second has 3 dots. The third has 9 dots. Each figure is 3 times the size of the figure before it. The next figure will be three of the last figure:

A figure that includes three of the last figure has 3 · 9 = 27 dots.

Patterns in fact families

A fact family is the set of equations that use the same three numbers in the original equation.

Multiplication and division
Write the fact family for each equation. The equations will contain either multiplication or division.

    1) 4 · 3 = 12
    2) 8 · 9 = 72
    3) 12 ÷ 6 = 2

    1) 4 · 3 = 12
    3 · 4 = 12
    12 ÷ 3 = 4
    12 ÷ 4 = 3

    2) 8 · 9 = 72
    9 · 8 = 72
    72 ÷ 9 = 8
    72 ÷ 8 = 9

    3) 12 ÷ 6 = 2
    12 ÷ 2 = 6
    2 · 6 = 12
    6 · 2 = 12

Addition and subtraction

Write the fact family for each equation. The equations will contain either addition or subtraction.

1) 10 + 6 = 16
2) 23 – 9 = 14
3) 8 + 30 = 38

1) 10 + 6 = 16
6 + 10 = 16
16 – 6 = 10
16 – 10 = 6

2) 23 – 9 = 14
23 – 14 = 9
14 + 9 = 23
9 + 14 = 23

3) 8 + 30 = 38
30 + 8 = 38
38 – 8 = 30
38 – 30 = 8

Table of paired numbers

Example 1

Each student is wearing two shoes. Create a table showing the total number of shoes for: 1, 2, 3, 4, and 5 students.

Number of students	Total number of shoes
1	2
2	4
3	6
4	8
5	10

Example 2

A tricycle has three wheels. Create a table showing the total number of wheels for: 1, 2, 3, 4, and 5 tricycles.

Number of tricycles	Total number of wheels
1	3
2	6
3	9
4	12
5	15

<u>Example 3</u>

Mr. Watson's class sells wrapping paper to raise money for a trip. Each roll of wrapping paper is sold for $6. They start the following table to record the total money earned.

Number of rolls	Total money earned
10	$60
20	$120
30	$180

Write a table showing the total money earned if 40 or 50 rolls are sold.

In the table, as the number of rolls increases by 10, the total money earned increases by $60. To find the total money earned if 40 rolls are sold, add $60 to the total money earned if 30 rolls are sold. To find the total money earned if 50 rolls are sold, add $60 to the total money earned if 40 rolls are sold.

Number of rolls	Total money earned
10	$60
20	$120
30	$180
40	$180 + $60 = $240
50	$240 + $60 = $300

Geometry and Spatial Reasoning

A triangle has three sides that can be of varying lengths.

A square is a quadrilateral where all side lengths and angle measures are equal.

A pentagon is a five sided polygon.

A hexagon is a six sided polygon, if all angles and sides are equal then it is a regular hexagon.

An octagon has eight equal length sides.

Three dimensional figures

The following are descriptions of three-dimensional figures:

A pyramid has a polygon base and triangular sides that meet at a single point.

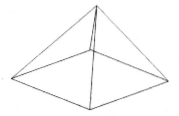

A cone has only one base, which is a circle, and a single vertex opposite the base.

A prism has two congruent, parallel bases that are polygons. The sides of a prism are parallelograms.

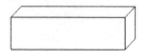

A cylinder has two congruent, parallel bases that are circles or ovals.

Rectangular prism

A rectangular prism is a three-dimensional figure with sides that are all rectangles.

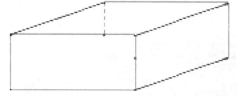

- 14 -

Congruency

Congruent figures are the same size and shape. This means that all of the sides are the same length, and all of the angles are the same measure. The two rectangles below are congruent.

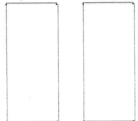

Congruent parts of a square

The congruent parts are the parts of the square that are the same size. On a square, all side lengths are equal and all angles are equal. The congruent parts are the side and angles. For example:

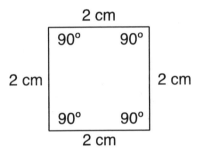

Congruent parts of a parallelogram

A parallelogram is a quadrilateral where pairs of opposite sides are parallel. Opposite sides of a parallelogram are congruent, and opposite angles are also congruent. For example:

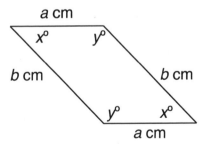

Congruent triangle

Example 1

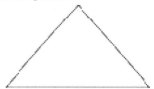

A congruent triangle can be made by moving the original triangle left, right, up, or down. The congruent figure below, with the dashed lines, was moved up and to the right.

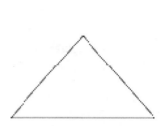

Example 2
Create a congruent triangle to the one below by turning the triangle.

To create a congruent triangle by rotating, first draw a point of rotation. The point can be outside, inside, or on the figure. Then pick a number of degrees to rotate the figure. For example, rotate the figure 90°.

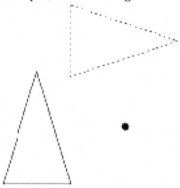

Symmetry

If a figure has symmetry, a line of symmetry can be drawn in the figure. On either side of the line of symmetry, the pieces of the figure are congruent.
For example:

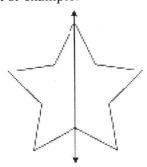

<u>Example</u>
Find the line of symmetry for the figure below:

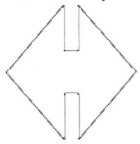

On either side of the line of symmetry, the pieces of the figure are congruent. A line of symmetry can be drawn horizontally through the middle of the figure. A line of symmetry could also be drawn vertically through the middle of the figure:

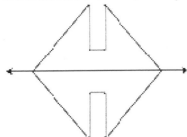

Number line

Example 1
Name each point on the number line below:

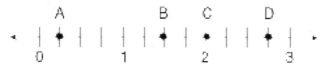

Use the dashed lines on the number line to identify each point. Each dashed line between two whole numbers is $\frac{1}{4}$. The line halfway between two numbers is $\frac{1}{2}$.

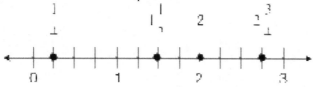

Example 2
Put the following numbers on a number line: 4, $5\frac{3}{4}$, $6\frac{1}{2}$, 7.

Create a number line and draw dashed lines between whole numbers to represent $\frac{1}{4}$. The line halfway between two numbers is $\frac{1}{2}$.

- 18 -

Measurement

Length of a segment

Find the length of the line segment using the ruler below. The ruler is in inches.

The line segment begins at 0, and ends at the mark that is halfway between 1 and 2 inches. Halfway between 1 and 2 inches is $1\frac{1}{2}$ inches. The line segment is $1\frac{1}{2}$ inches long.

Perimeter

Rectangle
A rectangle has a length of 3 units and a width of 1 unit. Find the perimeter of the rectangle.

Draw a model of the rectangle with the given side lengths.

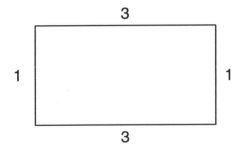

The perimeter of a rectangle is the sum of side lengths: perimeter = 3 units + 1 unit + 3 units + 1 unit = 8 units.

Triangle
A triangle has sides that are 6, 8, and 11 units long. Find the perimeter of the triangle.

Draw a model of the triangle with the given side lengths. The lengths of the sides do not have to exactly match the given measurements, but each side should be labeled.

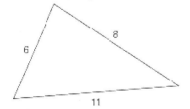

The perimeter is the sum of the side lengths: 6 units + 8 units + 11 units = 25 units.

Area

Rectangle
Draw a rectangle that is 8 units high and 10 units wide.

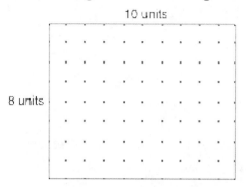

To find the area, count the squares inside the area of the rectangle. There are 80 squares; the area of the rectangle is 80 units^2.

Square
Draw a square that is 7 units wide and 7 units high. Here, each circle represents one unit.

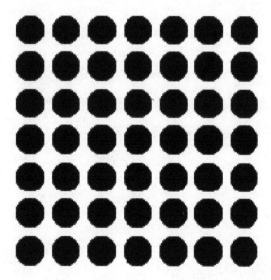

The total number of circles is the area. There are 49 circles, so the area of the square is 49 units^2.

Temperature

Find the temperature, in degrees Fahrenheit, on the thermometer below:

The temperature on the thermometer is halfway between 70° and 80°. The temperature halfway between 70° and 80° is 75° F.

Time

<u>Example 1</u>
Draw the time 7:20 on an analog clock and a digital clock.

On the analog clock, the small hand will be just after the 7, showing it is just after 7 o'clock. The big hand will be at 20 minutes, which is at 4.

On a digital clock, the time will be written in the order *hours, then minutes*. Since the hour is only one digit, there may be a 0 before the 7.

- 21 -

Example 2
Find the time on the clock below.

The big hand is on the 11, so the minutes is 55. The small hand is just before the 1, which means that it is close to 1 o'clock, but it is not yet 1 o'clock. It is still the 12 o'clock hour. The time is 12:55.

Probability and Statistics

Bar graph

<u>Example 1</u>
A class records data when students are born. Draw a bar graph to represent the data in the table below.

Month born	Number of students	Month born	Number of students
January	3	July	1
February	5	August	0
March	2	September	4
April	1	October	6
May	0	November	5
June	4	December	3

To draw a bar graph, first create horizontal and vertical axes. The horizontal axis will be the month, and the vertical axis will be the number of students. Draw rectangles at each month, showing the number of students born in each month.

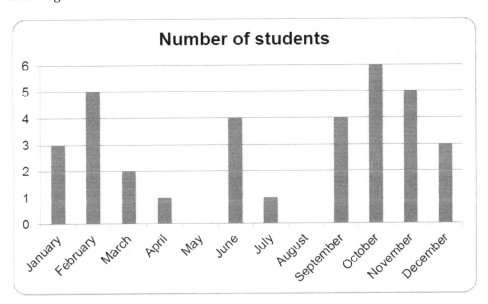

<u>Example 2</u>
List the types of pet in order of most popular to least popular.

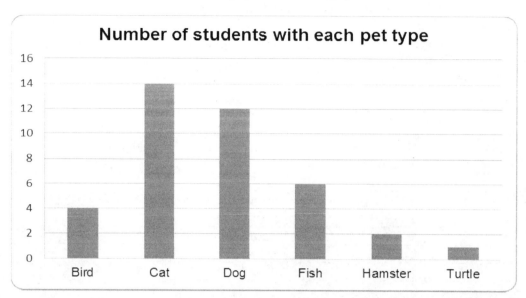

The pet with the highest number of students is the most popular. 14 students have cats, 12 students have dogs, 6 students have fish, 4 have birds, 2 have hamsters, and 1 has a turtle. From most to least popular the pets are: cats, dogs, fish, birds, hamsters, and turtle.

Pictograph

A pictograph is a graph that uses images to represent the data. It is similar to a bar graph, except instead of bars it uses images. For example, a pictograph may use an image of an apple to represent the number of apples a shop sold each month. The months would be listed on the vertical axis with apples going out horizontally to represent the number of apples sold that month.

Example

A basketball team wants to compare their average number of points per game, and they decide to draw a pictograph to represent the data. Use the pictograph to answer the questions.

a) Who is more likely to score at least 15 points in a game?
b) Who is least likely to score at least 15 points in a game?
c) Which two players are equally likely to score 15 points in a game?

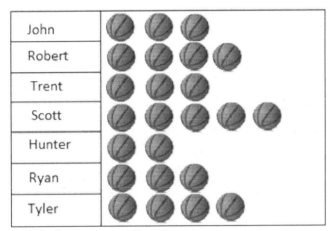

Each ball represents 3 points

a) The player most likely to score 15 points in a game is Scott. Scott has five basketballs by his name which means he averages 15 points a game.
b) The player least likely to score 15 points a game is Hunter. Hunter has two basketballs by his name which means he only averages six points a game.
c) The only two players with the same average are Robert and Tyler. They are each equally as likely to score 15 points in a game.

Mathematics Practice Test #1

Practice Questions

1. Jillian writes the number: 860,002. Which of the following represents this number, in words?

Ⓐ Eight hundred sixty thousand, twenty

Ⓑ Eight hundred sixty thousand, two

Ⓒ Eight hundred sixty two thousand

Ⓓ Eight hundred six thousand, two

2. Arlan compares his annual electricity expenses over a five-year time span. His annual expenses are shown in the table below.

Year	Expense
2007	$1,224
2008	$1,319
2009	$1,046
2010	$1,529
2011	$1,342

Which of the following shows the years listed, in order, from lowest electricity expense to highest electricity expense?

Ⓐ 2009, 2008, 2007, 2010, 2011

Ⓑ 2007, 2009, 2011, 2010, 2008

Ⓒ 2009, 2007, 2011, 2008, 2010

Ⓓ 2009, 2007, 2008, 2011, 2010

- 26 -

3. Steve had to pay a library fee. The amount he paid is shown below.

How much did he pay?

   Ⓐ $2.84

   Ⓑ $2.59

   Ⓒ $2.74

   Ⓓ $2.69

4. Wyatt's coach passed out balls to the entire team. One-third of the balls Wyatt received were basketballs. Which of the following could represent the balls he received?

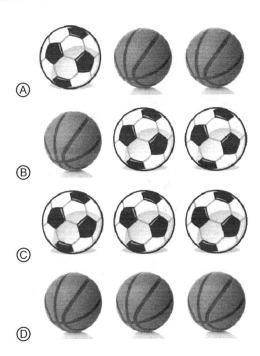

- 27 -

5. An author had a book published last year. The number of books sold each month, for the first six months are: 321, 452, 608, 381, 294, and 458.
Which of the following lists the number of books sold each month, in order from greatest to least?

Ⓐ 608, 452, 458, 321, 384, 294

Ⓑ 452, 458, 608, 381, 321, 294

Ⓒ 458, 608, 452, 381, 321, 294

Ⓓ 608, 458, 452, 381, 321, 294

6. Students were given triangles and hexagons to be used during a class activity. One-third of the shapes each student received were triangles. Which of the following could represent the number of triangles and number of hexagons each student received?

7. What number sentence is illustrated by the diagram below?

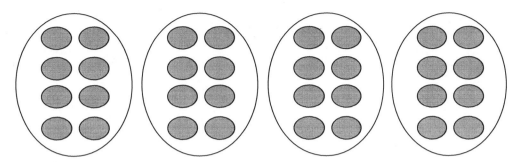

    Ⓐ $32 \times 4 = 128$

    Ⓑ $32 - 4 = 28$

    Ⓒ $32 \div 4 = 8$

    Ⓓ $32 + 4 = 36$

8. Solve and place answer on the provided griddable sheet.

96
× 8

9. Edward ascends to the top of a mountain over the course of two days. On Friday, he ascends 482 feet. He ascends another 362 feet on Saturday. How many feet did he ascend in all?

    Ⓐ 848 feet

    Ⓑ 836 feet

    Ⓒ 840 feet

    Ⓓ 844 feet

10. Kristen must buy three items that are priced at $4.58, $6.22, and $8.94. What is the best estimate for the total cost of all three items?

    Ⓐ $18

    Ⓑ $16

    Ⓒ $20

    Ⓓ $22

11. Which of the following represents $\frac{2}{3}$?

Ⓐ

Ⓑ

Ⓒ

Ⓓ

12. On Monday, David finished gluing 96 tiles in 8 hours. On Tuesday, he finished gluing 72 tiles in 8 hours. Which of the following is a possible first step in determining how many more tiles he glued per hour on Monday?

Ⓐ Add the number of tiles glued each day

Ⓑ Subtract the number of hours it took to glue the tiles from the number of tiles glued

Ⓒ Multiply the number of hours spent gluing tiles on Monday by the number of hours spent gluing tiles on Tuesday

Ⓓ Divide the number of tiles glued each day by the number of hours it took to glue them

13. Solve and place answer on the provided griddable sheet.
At the birthday party, each guest received 12 game tokens and each game takes 2 tokens. If there were 12 guests at the party, estimate how many games were played (to the nearest tens)?

14. What is the eighth number in the pattern: 321, 329, 337, 345, ___, ___, ___, ___?

Ⓐ 369

Ⓑ 385

Ⓒ 377

Ⓓ 353

- 30 -

15. A little boy has three nickels, four dimes, two pennies, and two quarters. How much money does he have?

   Ⓐ $1.00

   Ⓑ $0.90

   Ⓒ $1.07

   Ⓓ $100

16. James drew the following connected squares and labeled them as Figure 1, Figure 2, and so on.

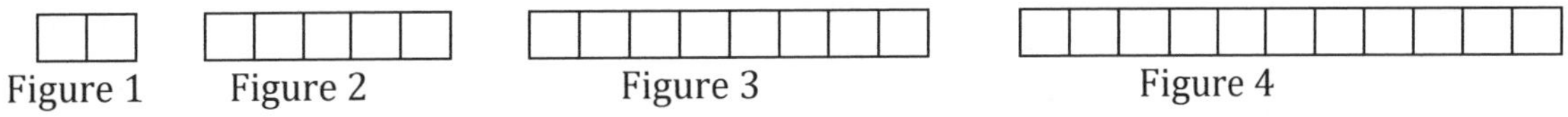

Figure 1   Figure 2   Figure 3   Figure 4

If he continues this pattern, how many squares will he use for Figure 9?

   Ⓐ 21

   Ⓑ 23

   Ⓒ 26

   Ⓓ 29

17. A teacher donates to a local charity. Each year, she donates three times the amount donated the previous year. If the teacher donated $2 the first year, how much did she donate during the fifth year?

   Ⓐ $158

   Ⓑ $164

   Ⓒ $162

   Ⓓ $144

18. Solve and place answer on the provided griddable sheet.
One number can correctly fill in all the blank boxes below. What is that number?

   $? \times 3 = 12$

   $16 - ? = 12$

   $8 + ? = 12$

19. A class collects spiders. Spiders have 8 legs each. Which table shows the number of legs found on the spiders brought to class?

Ⓐ

Number of Spiders	Number of Legs
2	10
3	11
6	14
8	16
11	19

Ⓑ

Number of Spiders	Number of Legs
4	28
5	35
9	63
12	84
14	98

Ⓒ

Number of Spiders	Number of Legs
3	12
4	13
8	17
10	19
12	21

Ⓓ

Number of Spiders	Number of Legs
3	24
5	40
6	48
9	72
12	96

20. The total number of candy pieces found in different numbers of candy jars is shown in the table below.

Number of Candy Jars	Number of Candy Pieces
2	28
4	56
5	70
9	126

How many candy pieces are there in 13 candy jars?

    Ⓐ 154

    Ⓑ 168

    Ⓒ 182

    Ⓓ 196

21. Penny drinks 8 glasses of water each day. The number of glasses of water she drinks over a 12-day time span can be determined, using the number sentence:
$8 \times 12 = ?$
Which number sentence would not show the number of glasses of water she drinks?

    Ⓐ $? \div 8 = 12$

    Ⓑ $12 \times 8 = ?$

    Ⓒ $? \div 12 = 8$

    Ⓓ $12 - 8 = ?$

22. Belinda draws a rectangle with a length of 6 cm. She draws a second rectangle with a length of 11 cm. Belinda continues drawing more rectangles, where for each rectangle drawn, she uses a length that is 5 more centimeters than the length of the previous rectangle. If this pattern continues, what will be the length of the 11th rectangle?

    Ⓐ 46 cm

    Ⓑ 54 cm

    Ⓒ 56 cm

    Ⓓ 61 cm

23. What is the next number in the series shown?
    132, 123, 115, 108, 102

Ⓐ 82

Ⓑ 87

Ⓒ 92

Ⓓ 97

24. Which of the following figures is NOT congruent to the others shown?

Ⓐ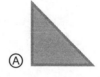

Ⓑ

Ⓒ

Ⓓ

25. Which number is greater than the number shown by Point M on the number line?

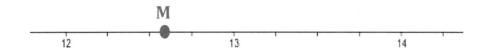

   Ⓐ 12 ¼

   Ⓑ 12 ½

   Ⓒ 12

   Ⓓ 12 ¾

26. Which figure has more than 9 edges?

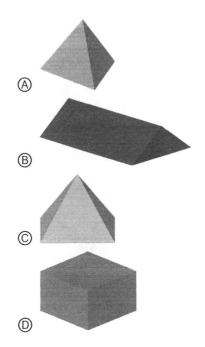

27. Which shape has a number of vertices that is equal to two times the number of vertices found on a triangle?

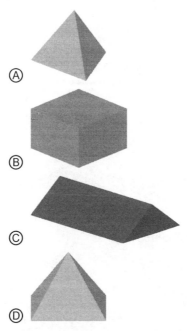

Ⓐ

Ⓑ

Ⓒ

Ⓓ

28. Which shape has the most faces?

Ⓐ Square pyramid

Ⓑ Triangular prism

Ⓒ Cube

Ⓓ Triangular pyramid

29. Which of the following is congruent to the shape shown below?

Ⓐ

Ⓑ

Ⓒ

Ⓓ

30. How many lines of symmetry does the trapezoid shown below have?

Ⓐ 0

Ⓑ 1

Ⓒ 2

Ⓓ 3

- 37 -

31. What number does Point P represent?

Ⓐ $10\frac{1}{4}$

Ⓑ $10\frac{1}{2}$

Ⓒ $10\frac{1}{3}$

Ⓓ $10\frac{3}{4}$

32. Which of the following shapes has 5 fewer lines of symmetry than an octagon?

Ⓐ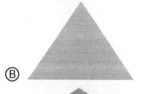

Ⓑ

Ⓒ

Ⓓ

- 38 -

33. What is the perimeter of the triangle shown below?

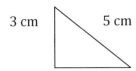

3 cm   5 cm

4 cm

(A) 6 cm

(B) 12 cm

(C) 9 cm

(D) 8 cm

34. What is the perimeter of the trapezoid shown below?

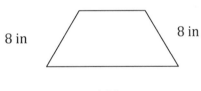

3 in

8 in   8 in

14 in

(A) 28 in

(B) 31 in

(C) 34 in

(D) 33 in

35. Which of the following is the best estimate for the distance from the center of the circle, marked C, to a point on the circle?

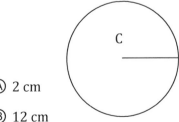

C

(A) 2 cm

(B) 12 cm

(C) 5 cm

(D) 8 cm

36. A crayon is shown below. Use the ruler from your mathematics chart to measure the length of the crayon. About how long is the crayon, from base to tip, to the nearest inch?

Ⓐ 2 in

Ⓑ 3 in

Ⓒ 4 in

Ⓓ 5 in

37. How many square units are found in the trapezoid below?

Ⓐ 8 square units

Ⓑ 12 square units

Ⓒ 10 square units

Ⓓ 9 square units

38. What is the approximate temperature shown on the thermometer, in degrees Fahrenheit?

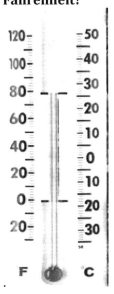

Ⓐ 0° F

Ⓑ 80° F

Ⓒ 30° F

Ⓓ 25° F

39. Karen goes to the library at the time shown on the clock below. At what time does she go to the library?

Ⓐ 8:10

Ⓑ 1:30

Ⓒ 6:10

Ⓓ 2:30

40. Which clock below would be read as a five o'clock?

Ⓐ 5:00

Ⓑ 5:30

Ⓒ 5:05

Ⓓ 5:55

41. Aubrey rolls a die. Which of the following statements is true?

Ⓐ She is more likely to roll a 3 than a 6

Ⓑ She is equally likely to roll a 3 or a 6

Ⓒ She is less likely to roll a 3 than a 6

Ⓓ She is certain to roll a 3 or a 6

42. The bar graph below shows the number of zoos found in four states.

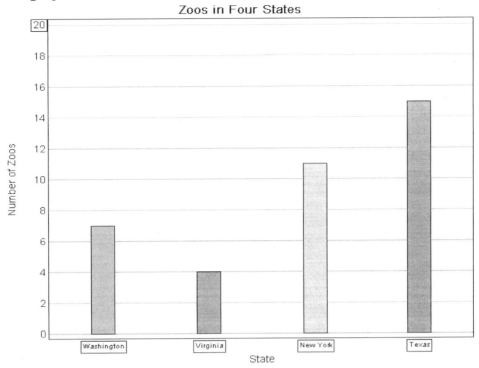

Which state has the most zoos?

Ⓐ Washington

Ⓑ Virginia

Ⓒ New York

Ⓓ Texas

43. A fish bowl contains 2 striped, 4 orange, and 2 blue fish. Eli randomly scoops a fish from the bowl. Which of the following statements is true?

Ⓐ He is less likely to scoop an orange than a striped fish

Ⓑ He is more likely to scoop a striped than a blue fish

Ⓒ He is more likely to scoop a blue than an orange fish

Ⓓ He is equally likely to scoop a striped and a blue fish

44. Which of the following events is certain?

Ⓐ Rolling a 7 on a die

Ⓑ Rolling an even number on a die

Ⓒ Rolling a number less than 8 on a die

Ⓓ Rolling an odd number on a die

45. The bar graph below shows the favorite sport of the students in the class.

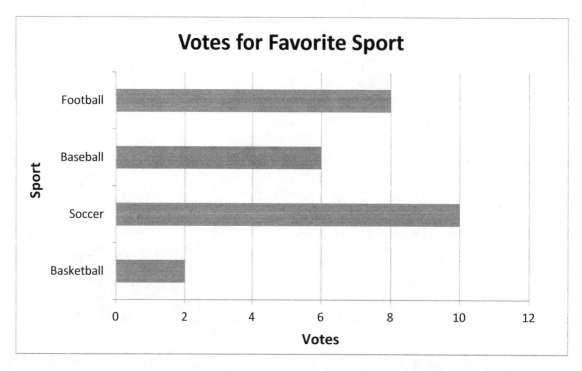

How many fewer votes did basketball get compared to baseball?

Ⓐ 2

Ⓑ 3

Ⓒ 4

Ⓓ 5

46. The number of lawns, finished by four different landscaping companies, in one week, is shown in the table below.

Landscaping Company	Number of Lawns
Landscaping Company A	12
Landscaping Company B	18
Landscaping Company C	6
Landscaping Company D	16

Which pictograph shows the number of lawns finished by each company?

Ⓐ Each tree represents 2 lawns.

Company A: 🌳🌳🌳🌳🌳🌳

Company B: 🌳🌳🌳🌳🌳🌳🌳🌳🌳

Company C: 🌳🌳🌳

Company D: 🌳🌳🌳🌳🌳🌳🌳🌳

Ⓑ Each tree represents 4 lawns.

Company A: 🌳🌳🌳🌳

Company B: 🌳🌳🌳🌳🌳🌳

Company C: 🌳🌳

Company D: 🌳🌳🌳🌳🌳

Ⓒ Each tree represents 2 lawns.

Company A: 🌳🌳🌳

Company B: 🌳🌳🌳🌳

Company C: 🌳🌳

Company D: 🌳🌳🌳🌳🌳

Ⓓ Each tree represents 3 lawns.

Company A: 🌳🌳🌳🌳🌳🌳

Company B: 🌳🌳🌳🌳🌳🌳🌳🌳

Company C: 🌳🌳🌳

Company D: 🌳🌳🌳🌳🌳🌳🌳🌳

Answers and Explanations

TEKS Standard §111.5(b)(1)(D)

1. B: The number, 860,002 has an 8 in the hundred-thousands place, a 6 in the ten-thousands place, a 0 in the thousands place, a 0 in the hundreds place, a 0 in the tens place, and a 2 in the ones place. The 860 written in front of the comma represents, "Eight hundred sixty thousand." The 2 in the ones place represents, "Two." Therefore, the number is read, "Eight hundred sixty thousand, two."

TEKS Standard §111.5(b)(2)(D)

2. D: The annual expenses for Years 2009, 2007, 2008, 2011, and 2010 are $1,046, $1,224, $1,319, $1,342, and $1,529, respectively. These amounts are listed in order from lowest to highest. Since all of the numbers have a 1 in the thousands place, the numerals in the hundreds place must be compared. For the amounts of $1,319 and $1,342, the numerals in the tens place must be compared. No other choice shows the years listed in increasing order of expense.

TEKS Standard §111.5(b)(4)(C)

3. C: There are 2 dollar bills, which represent 2 dollars. There are also 2 quarters, 2 nickels, 1 dime, and 4 pennies. Two quarters are worth $0.50 since each is worth $0.25 $(2 \times 0.25 = 0.50)$, 2 nickels are worth $0.10 since each is worth $0.05 $(2 \times 0.05 = 0.10)$, 1 dime is worth $0.10, and 4 pennies are worth $0.04 since each is worth $0.01. The sum of the coins can be found by writing: $0.50 + $0.10 + $0.10 + $0.04, which equals $0.74. The sum of the two dollar bills and the coins can be written as: $2.00 + $0.74. Thus, he paid $2.74.

TEKS Standard §111.5(b)(3)(A)

4. B: If 1/3 of the balls Wyatt received were basketballs that means the remaining balls he received must have been soccer balls. Since the fraction used is 1/3, look at it as if he received 3 balls. One ball was a basketball and the remaining balls had to be soccer balls. This is now a simple subtraction problem. 3 − 1 = 2 soccer balls.

TEKS Standard §111.5(b)(2)(D)

5. D: The numbers: 608, 458, 452, 381, 321, and 294 are written in order from greatest to least. An examination of the numerals in the hundreds place reveals that 608 is the greatest and 294 is the least. The numbers, 458 and 452, are greater than the numbers, 381 and 321, based on the value of the digits in the hundreds place. An examination of the numerals in the ones place, since both the digits in the hundreds and the tens places are the same, allows you to compare 458 and 452, which shows 458 to be the larger number. An examination of the numerals in the tens place allows you to compare 381 and 321, since the digits in the hundreds place are the same, which shows 381 to be the larger number. None of the other choices show the numbers in descending order.

TEKS Standard §111.5(b)(3)(A)

6. C: Choice C shows 2 triangles and 4 hexagons, which is a total of 6 shapes. The fraction 2 out of 6, or $\frac{2}{6}$, also represents 1 out of 3, or $\frac{1}{3}$. None of the other choices represent this fraction: Choice A shows $\frac{3}{6}$, which equals $\frac{1}{2}$. Choice B shows $\frac{1}{4}$. Choice D shows $\frac{1}{6}$.

TEKS Standard §111.5(b)(4)(E)

7. C: The diagram shows 32 counters divided into 4 groups, with 8 counters in each group. Therefore, the total number of counters, 32, is divided by 4, giving a quotient of 8, which is written as: $32 \div 4 = 8$.

TEKS Standard §111.5(b)(4)(G)

8. This is a simple multiplication problem which involves carrying the excess (greater than a single digit) to the next column. Start with the 8 and multiply each digit above: 8 x 6 = 48. Write down the 8 and place the 4 on top of the 9. Multiply 8 x 9 to get 72. Add in the 4 to get 76. Write down the number 76 and the product is **768**.

TEKS Standard §111.5(b)(4)(A)

9. D: The total number of feet he ascended can be determined by adding 482 feet and 362 feet. The sum of 482 and 362 is 844. Thus, he ascended 844 feet in all.

TEKS Standard §111.5(b)(4)(B)

10. C: The item priced at $4.58 can be rounded to $5. The item priced at $6.22 can be rounded to $6. The item priced at $8.94 can be rounded to $9. The sum of 5, 6 and 9 is 20. Thus, the best estimate is $20.

TEKS Standard §111.5(b)(3)(A)

11. B: Choice B shows 4 shaded sections out of 6 total sections. The fraction, $\frac{4}{6}$, is the same as the fraction, $\frac{2}{3}$. Two shaded sections represent one-third of the total. Thus, four shaded sections represent two-thirds of the total. Each of the pictures has 6 total sections, so the other choices can be written as fractions with a 6 in the denominator. Choice A shows $\frac{3}{6}$, which equals $\frac{1}{2}$. Choice C shows . Choice D shows $\frac{2}{6}$, which equals $\frac{1}{3}$. So, only Choice B shows the correct picture.

TEKS Standard §111.5(b)(4)(K)

12. D: A possible first step would be to divide the number of tiles glued each day by the number of hours it took to glue the tiles. The two quotients would then represent approximately how many tiles glued per hour, and could then be compared.

TEKS Standard §111.5(b)(4)(B) and (4)(K)

13. Begin with the tokens given to each guest, which was 12. But the problem states that every game takes two tokens, so each guest can play only 6 games, not 12. Multiply this by the number of guests, 12, to equal 72 games. Round this number to the nearest tens to get **70**.

TEKS Standard §111.5(b)(5)

14. C: Each number is 8 more than the previous number, which means that the next number can be found by adding 8 to the previous number. Thus, the fifth number is 353, the sixth number is 361, the seventh number is 369, and the eighth number is 377.

TEKS Standard §111.5(b)(4)(C)

15. C: Convert the coins to cents and apply addition. Each nickel is worth 5 cents, so 3 nickels equals 15 cents. Each dime is worth 10 cents, so 4 dimes equals 40 cents. Each penny is worth 1 cent, so 2 pennies equals 2 cents. A quarter is worth 25 cents, so 2 quarters equals 50 cents.. 15 + 40 + 2 + 50 = 107 cents. Since there are 100 cents in a dollar, this becomes 1 dollar with 7 cents remaining or $1.07

TEKS Standard §111.5(b)(5)

16. C: Each figure has 3 more squares than the previous figure, so adding 3 to the number of squares in the previous figure yields the number of squares in the next figure. Thus, he will use 14 squares for Figure 5, 17 squares for Figure 6, 20 squares for Figure7, 23 squares for Figure 8, and 26 squares for Figure 9.

TEKS Standard §111.5(b)(5)(B)

17. C: In order to find the amount donated the following year, you multiply the amount donated the previous year by 3. Thus, the amount donated the second year was $6 ($2 × 3). The amount donated the third year was $18 ($6 × 3). The amount donated the fourth year was $54 ($18 × 3). The amount donated the fifth year was $162 ($54 × 3).

TEKS Standard §111.5(b)(5)(D) and (4)(A)

18. The correct answer is **4**. 4 X 3 = 12; 16 − 4 =12, and 8 + 4 = 12.

TEKS Standard §111.5(b)(4)(K)

19. D: Each spider has 8 legs. In order to find the number of legs present with 3 spiders, you multiply 3 by 8, which is 24. Thus, 3 spiders have 24 legs in all. Choice D is the only table that shows each number of spiders, multiplied by 8, to yield the correct product representing the total number of legs.

TEKS Standard §111.5(b)(4)(K)

20. C: Each candy jar has 14 pieces of candy. This can be determined by dividing the number of pieces of candy by the number of candy jars: $28 \div 2 = 14, 56 \div 4 = 14, 70 \div 5 = 14, 126 \div 9 = 14$. Since the data in the table shows that there are 14 pieces of candy in each jar, multiplying $13 \times 14 = 182$ finds the total number of pieces of candy that are in 13 candy jars.

TEKS Standard §111.5(b)(4)(K)

21. D: If she drinks 8 glasses of water each day, the number of glasses of water she drinks in 12 days can be determined by multiplying 8 by 12. This product is 96; thus she drinks 96 glasses of water in a 12-day time span. The relationship between the number of glasses of water she drinks per day and the total number of glasses of water she drinks in 12 days can be represented by an appropriate multiplication or division number sentence within the following fact family: $8 \times 12 = 96, 96 \div 8 = 12, 12 \times 8 = 96, 96 \div 12 = 8$. Subtracting 8 from 12 will not reveal the number of glasses she drinks in a 12-day time span. The number sentence: $12 - 8 = ?$, is not in this fact family.

TEKS Standard §111.5 (b)(5)

22. C: If each rectangle has a length that is 5 cm more than that of the previous rectangle, the lengths of the 3rd rectangle through the 11th rectangle can be found by adding 5 cm to the length of the second triangle and continuing for each next rectangle. So, the lengths of the rectangles will be as follows: 16 cm, 21 cm, 26 cm, 31 cm, 36 cm, 41 cm, 46 cm, 51 cm, and 56 cm.

TEKS Standard §111.5(b)(5)

23. D: The pattern is subtracting one less number each time:

132 – 9 = 123
123 – 8 = 115
115 – 7 = 108
108 – 6 = 102

The next number to be subtracted is 5, so 102 – 5 = 97

TEKS Standard §111.5(b)(6)

24. D: Choices A, B, and C are all the same right triangle just flipped around. Answer choice D is a different triangle and therefore not congruent.

TEKS Standard §111.5(b)(3)

25. D: 12 ¼ is represented by the first tick mark to the right of the 12. 12 ½ is the second tick mark and 12 ¾ is the third tick mark, or the tick mark before the 13. Only 12 ¾ appears to the right of point M on the number line, making it greater.

TEKS Standard §111.5(b)(6)(A)

26. D: An edge is the intersection of two faces. A triangular pyramid (Choice A) has 6 edges, while a triangular prism (Choice B) has 9 edges, a square pyramid (Choice C) has 8 edges, and a cube (Choice D) has 12 edges. The cube is the only figure with more than 9 edges.

TEKS Standard §111.5(b)(6)(A)

27. C: A vertex is a point where two or more edges meet. A triangle has 3 vertices. Two times that would be 6 vertices. The figure shown for Choice C is a triangular prism, which is the only figure that has 6 vertices. A triangular pyramid (Choice A) has 4 vertices, a cube (Choice B) has 8 vertices, and a square pyramid (Choice D) has 5 vertices.

TEKS Standard §111.5(b)(6)(A)

28. C: A cube (Choice C) has 6 faces, while a square pyramid and triangular prism (Choices A and B) each have 5 faces, and a triangular pyramid (Choice D) has 4 faces. So, a cube has the most faces out of these choices.

TEKS Standard §111.5(b)(6)

29. D: The trapezoid shown for Choice D is congruent to the given shape, provided. Basically, the shapes must be the same size to be congruent, but can be flipped or rotated in any way.

TEKS Standard §111.5(b)(6)(A)

30. B: The figure shown is an isosceles trapezoid, and it has 1 line of symmetry, which is a vertical line that passes through the midpoint of each base.

TEKS Standard §111.5(b)(3)(A)

31. B: Each increment represents one-half. This can be determined by counting that there are 3 marks, or 4 spaces, that lie between the difference of two wholes, as in between 10 and 12. Thus, one increment past 10, where Point P is located, represents $10\frac{1}{2}$.

- 49 -

TEKS Standard §111.5(b)(6)(A)

32. B: An octagon has 8 lines of symmetry, and 3 lines of symmetry is 5 fewer than 8 lines of symmetry. An equilateral triangle (Choice B) has 3 lines of symmetry, while a square (Choice A) has 4 lines of symmetry, a pentagon (Choice C) has 5 lines of symmetry, and an isosceles trapezoid (Choice D) has 1 line of symmetry. Thus, an equilateral triangle is the only shape shown that has 5 fewer lines of symmetry than an octagon.

TEKS Standard §111.5(b)(7)(B)

33. B: The distance around the triangle, or the perimeter, is equal to the sum of 3 cm, 5 cm, and 4 cm. Thus, the perimeter is 12 cm.

TEKS Standard §111.5(b)(7)(B)

34. D: The perimeter of the trapezoid is the distance around all of the sides, and is equal to the sum of 3 in, 8 in, 8 in, and 14 in. Thus, the perimeter is 33 in.

TEKS Standard §111.5(b)(6)

35. A: The distance from the center of the circle, marked C, to a point on the circle, is also known as the radius, and it is approximately 2 cm. The distance can be estimated by marking off estimated units of length for a centimeter. Such markings approximate 2 centimeters.

TEKS Standard §111.5(b)(7)

36. B: The crayon measures almost exactly 3 inches.

TEKS Standard §111.5(b)(6)

37. C: The trapezoid has 8 square units, plus 4 one-half square units, which equals 2 more square units. The sum of 8 square units and 2 square units is 10 square units.

TEKS Standard §111.5(b)(7)

38. B: The thermometer shows the temperature to be very close to 80 degrees Fahrenheit. It also shows the temperature in Celsius: about 25 degrees.

TEKS Standard §111.5(b)(7)

39. C: The short hand, or hour hand, is between 6 o'clock and 7 o'clock, revealing that Karen went to the library after 6 o'clock. The long hand, or minute hand, is pointed at the 2. Since the 2 on the clock represents 10 minutes after the hour (since each number shown on the clock represents 5 minutes and $2 \times 5 = 10$), the clock shows that Karen went to the library at 6:10.

TEKS Standard §111.5(b)(7)

40. A: Five o'clock shown on a digital clock would be shown as a 5 followed by two zeroes, indicating no minutes.

TEKS Standard §111.5(b)(8)

41. B: Since a die has one of each number, from 1 to 6, she is equally likely to roll any of the six numbers. The possibility of rolling one of these numbers is no more or less than the possibility of rolling another of these numbers. Thus, she is equally likely to roll a 3 or a 6.

TEKS Standard §111.5(b)(8)(B)

42. D: Texas has the most zoos because it has 15 zoos, while the other states each have 7 zoos, 4 zoos, and 11 zoos. Also, it can be seen from the graph that the bar representing Texas is much higher than the bars for the other states.

TEKS Standard §111.5(b)(8)

43. D: The more fish there is of a certain color the more likely it is that the color of fish is scooped. With more orange fish than striped fish in the bowl, he is more likely to scoop an orange fish than a striped one. There are equal amounts of striped and blue fish, so one is not more likely than the other. There are more orange fish than blue fish, so he is more likely to scoop an orange fish than a blue one.. Finally, the number of striped and blue fish is the same – so they are equally likely to be scooped compared to each other. Thus, Choice D is the only true statement.

TEKS Standard §111.5(b)(8)

44. C: A die has numbers 1 – 6, so rolling a number less than 8 is a certain occurrence. It will always happen. Choice A is incorrect because rolling a 7 would be impossible. Choices B and D are also incorrect because rolling either an even or odd number, since the die has both, would not be certain.

TEKS Standard §111.5(b)(8)(B)

45. C: Baseball received 6 votes and basketball received only 2 votes. The difference is 6 – 2 = 4 fewer votes.

TEKS Standard §111.5(b)(8)

46. A: Since each tree represents 2 lawns, the pictograph shows that the number of lawns finished by Company A is equal to 6 × 2, or 12 lawns, the number of lawns finished by Company B is equal to 9 × 2, or 18 lawns, the number of lawns finished by Company C is equal to 3 × 2, or 6 lawns, and the number of lawns finished by Company D is equal to 8 × 2, or 16 lawns. This is the only pictograph that represents the correct number of lawns.

Practice Questions

1. Which number is read as, "Two hundred four"?

Ⓐ 2004

Ⓑ 204

Ⓒ 240

Ⓓ 24

2. Which numbers are listed in order from least to greatest?

Ⓐ 539, 542, 528, 576, 588

Ⓑ 588, 576, 542, 539, 528

Ⓒ 528, 542, 539, 588, 576

Ⓓ 528, 539, 542, 576, 588

3. Which of the following is an expression for five subtracted from twenty-five equals twenty?

Ⓐ 25 - 20 = 5

Ⓑ 5 - 25 = 5

Ⓒ 25 – 5 = 20

Ⓓ 20 + 5 = 25

4. Camille's teacher passed out crayons and pencils to students in her class. One-fourth of the writing tools Camille received were crayons. Which of the following could represent the number of crayons she received?

Ⓐ

Ⓑ

Ⓒ

Ⓓ

5. Bercu sells 128 hot dogs this month. She sold 117 hot dogs last month. How many hot dogs has she sold in these past two months?

Ⓐ 235

Ⓑ 241

Ⓒ 242

Ⓓ 245

6. Chandler paid for a book at a book fare. He gave the clerk the amount of money shown below. How much money did he give the clerk?

Ⓐ $2.57

Ⓑ $2.72

Ⓒ $2.77

Ⓓ $2.82

7. What number sentence is shown by the diagram below?

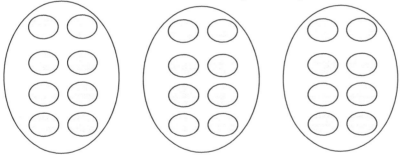

Ⓐ 24 × 3 = 72

Ⓑ 24 − 8 = 16

Ⓒ 24 + 8 = 32

Ⓓ 24 ÷ 3 = 8

8. Solve and place answer on the provided griddable sheet.

78
× 9

9. On Monday morning, a store manager gave 6 coupons to every customer who entered the store. If 89 people entered the store that morning, which is the best estimate for the total number of coupons the store manager gave to customers?

    Ⓐ 300

    Ⓑ 540

    Ⓒ 480

    Ⓓ 500

10. Farm A has 8 chickens and 3 horses. Farm B has 6 chickens and 5 horses. Which of the following is a possible first step in determining which farm contains more animal feet?

    Ⓐ Multiply the number of chickens on each farm by 2, and multiply the number of horses on each farm by 4

    Ⓑ Find the total number of animals found on both farms

    Ⓒ Multiply the sum of the number of chickens and horses, found on both farms, by 6

    Ⓓ Add 2 to the number of chickens found on each farm, and add 4 to the number of horses found on each farm

11. Which model shows a fraction that is more than 4 out of 7?

    Ⓐ

    Ⓑ

    Ⓒ

    Ⓓ

12. The number of miles Jacob has walked each year over the past five years is shown in the table below.

Year 1	691
Year 2	567
Year 3	144
Year 4	963
Year 5	221

Which sequence of years shows the number of miles he walked each year, listed in order from greatest to least?

    Ⓐ Year 2, Year 4, Year 5, Year 1, Year 3

    Ⓑ Year 4, Year 1, Year 2, Year 5, Year 3

    Ⓒ Year 1, Year 4, Year 2, Year 5, Year 3

    Ⓓ Year 3, Year 2, Year 5, Year 4, Year 1

13. A neighborhood contains 4 streets. Street 1 has 23 houses, Street 2 has 12 houses, and Street 3 has 34 houses. Estimate by rounding, how many houses are in this neighborhood?

Ⓐ 40

Ⓑ 50

Ⓒ 60

Ⓓ 70

14. A little girl has two nickels, two dimes, four pennies, and one quarter. How much money does she have?

Ⓐ 30 cents

Ⓑ 90 cents

Ⓒ 60 cents

Ⓓ 40 cents

15. What is the seventh number in the pattern below?
228, 235, 242, 249, ___, ___, ___

Ⓐ 269

Ⓑ 256

Ⓒ 270

Ⓓ 263

16. A farmer plants rows of corn each growing season. The table below shows the total number of rows of corn the farmer has planted after several seasons.

Season	Number of Rows
Season 2	34
Season 4	68
Season 6	102
Season 7	119
Season 10	

How many rows of corn will the farmer have planted by the end of Season 10?

Ⓐ 153

Ⓑ 170

Ⓒ 136

Ⓓ 168

17. Which is the best table to show the relationship of wheels to each type of cycle?

Ⓐ

Type of Cycle	Number of Wheels
Unicycle	1
Bicycle	2
Tricycle	3

Ⓑ

Type of Cycle	Number of Wheels
Tricycle	1
Bicycle	2
Unicycle	3

Ⓒ

Type of Cycle	Number of Wheels
Bicycle	1
Tricycle	2
Unicycle	3

Ⓓ

Type of Cycle	Number of Wheels
Unicycle	1
Tricycle	2
Bicycle	3

18. Anand has 45 stamps in his collection. He decides to give all of his stamps to 5 friends. He writes the number sentence below to find out how many stamps to give each friend, if each friend is to receive an equal amount.

$$45 \div 5 = ?$$

Which number sentence would NOT help him find the number of stamps to give each friend?

Ⓐ $? \times 5 = 45$

Ⓑ $45 - 5 = ?$

Ⓒ $45 \div ? = 5$

Ⓓ $5 \times ? = 4$

19. What is the next item in the pattern below?

Ⓐ

Ⓑ

Ⓒ

Ⓓ

20. Hannah builds the towers shown below, using square blocks.

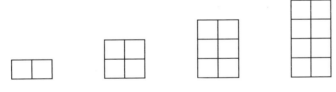

Tower 1   Tower 2   Tower 3   Tower 4

If she continues this pattern, how many square blocks will she use in the eighth tower?

Ⓐ 12

Ⓑ 16

Ⓒ 18

Ⓓ 14

21. The table below shows the number of books students brought to share with the class.

Number of Students	Number of Books
2	8
5	20
6	24
8	32

How many books did 12 students bring?

Ⓐ 44

Ⓑ 36

Ⓒ 40

Ⓓ 48

22. Which figure has 6 vertices?

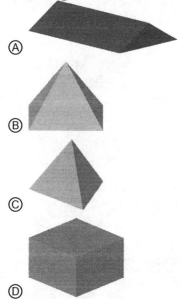

Ⓐ

Ⓑ

Ⓒ

Ⓓ

- 58 -

23. Jordan wants to show the number of wheels found on several cars. Which table should he use?

Ⓐ

Number of Cars	Number of Wheels
3	12
4	16
7	28
11	44
12	48

Ⓑ

Number of Cars	Number of Wheels
2	6
5	15
8	24
9	27
12	36

Ⓒ

Number of Cars	Number of Wheels
3	15
5	25
6	30
8	40
11	55

Ⓓ

Number of Cars	Number of Wheels
4	8
6	12
9	18
12	24
14	28

24. Which shape has more lines of symmetry than the one shown below?

Ⓐ

Ⓑ

Ⓒ

Ⓓ

25. Which number is greater than the number shown by Point S on the number line?

Ⓐ $14\frac{1}{4}$

Ⓑ 14

Ⓒ $14\frac{3}{4}$

Ⓓ $14\frac{1}{2}$

- 60 -

26. What statement is NOT true about the figure below?

(A) It has 5 vertices

(B) It has 6 edges

(C) It is a pyramid

(D) It has 5 faces

27. Which of the following is congruent to the triangle shown below?

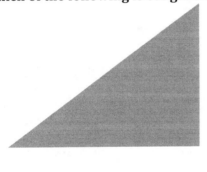

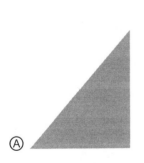
(A)

(C)

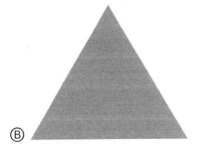
(B)

(D)

- 61 -

28. Which of the following figures has fewer than 5 faces?

Ⓐ Triangular pyramid

Ⓑ Triangular prism

Ⓒ Cube

Ⓓ Rectangular pyramid

29. Which figure does not have a line of symmetry?

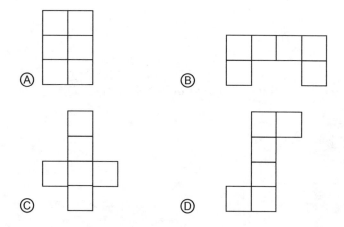

Ⓐ

Ⓑ

Ⓒ

Ⓓ

30. Ashley states, "All two-dimensional shapes are polygons." Which of the following shapes proves this statement to be false?

Ⓐ Triangles

Ⓑ Rectangles

Ⓒ Circles

Ⓓ Hexagons

31. Given the shapes below, which of the following sentences describes a characteristic common to all three shapes?

Ⓐ They are all prisms

Ⓑ They all have 5 faces

Ⓒ They are all pyramids

Ⓓ They all have at least 6 edges

32. What is the perimeter of the pentagon shown below?

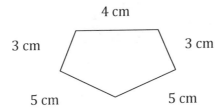

Ⓐ 29 cm

Ⓑ 20 cm

Ⓒ 15 cm

Ⓓ 25 cm

33. A student compares the perimeter of a triangle, a square, a rectangle, and a hexagon. The triangle has side lengths of 3 cm, 5 cm, and 6 cm. The square has a side length of 4 cm. The rectangle has a length of 3 cm and a width of 4 cm. The hexagon has six equal side lengths of 2 cm. Which of these shapes has the largest perimeter?

Ⓐ Triangle

Ⓑ Square

Ⓒ Rectangle

Ⓓ Hexagon

34. A pencil is shown below. Use the ruler from your mathematics chart to measure the length of the pencil. About how long is the pencil, from base to tip, to the nearest inch?

Ⓐ 2 in

Ⓑ 3 in

Ⓒ 4 in

Ⓓ 5 in

35. About how wide is the drawing of the notebook shown below?

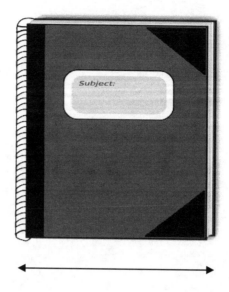

Ⓐ 2 cm

Ⓑ 3 cm

Ⓒ 5 cm

Ⓓ 7 cm

36. How many square units are found in the shape below?

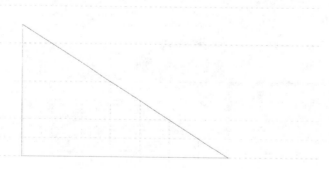

Ⓐ 23 square units

Ⓑ 23 $\frac{1}{2}$ square units

Ⓒ 24 square units

Ⓓ 24 $\frac{1}{2}$ square units

37. Solve and place answer on the provided griddable sheet.
A rectangle has a width of 7cm and a length of 9cm. What is its perimeter?

38. The outside temperature, on a spring day, in Flagstaff, Arizona, is shown on the thermometer below.

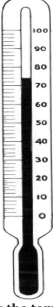

What is the temperature, in degrees Fahrenheit?

Ⓐ 77° F

Ⓑ 76° F

Ⓒ 79° F

Ⓓ 74° F

39. Amanda arrives at a birthday party at the time shown on the clock below.

What time did she arrive at the party?

Ⓐ 10:10

Ⓑ 2:10

Ⓒ 9:10

Ⓓ 2:50

40. Which clock below would be read as a quarter past three?

3:25

Ⓐ ▬▬▬▬▬▬▬▬▬▬

3:15

Ⓑ ▬▬▬▬▬▬▬▬▬▬

3:45

Ⓒ ▬▬▬▬▬▬▬▬▬▬

3:30

Ⓓ ▬▬▬▬▬▬▬▬▬▬

41. A bag contains 3 red cards, 7 blue cards, 9 green cards, and 6 yellow cards. Jesse randomly draws a card from the bag. Which of the following statements is true?

Ⓐ He is less likely to draw a green card than a yellow card

Ⓑ He is more likely to draw a yellow card than a red card

Ⓒ He is more likely to draw a yellow card than a blue card

Ⓓ He is equally likely to draw a red, blue, green, or yellow card

42. The number of cakes baked in one month, by different bakeries, is shown in the table below.

Bakery	Number of Cakes Baked
Bakery A	25
Bakery B	15
Bakery C	35
Bakery D	20

Which pictograph shows the number of cakes baked by each bakery?

Ⓐ Each picture of a cake represents 5 cakes.

Bakery A: 🎂 🎂 🎂 🎂 🎂

Bakery B: 🎂 🎂 🎂

Bakery C: 🎂 🎂 🎂 🎂 🎂 🎂 🎂

Bakery D: 🎂 🎂 🎂 🎂

Ⓑ Each picture of a cake represents 4 cakes.

Bakery A: 🎂 🎂 🎂 🎂 🎂 🎂

Bakery B: 🎂 🎂 🎂 🎂

Bakery C: 🎂 🎂 🎂 🎂 🎂 🎂 🎂 🎂 🎂

Bakery D: 🎂 🎂 🎂 🎂 🎂

Ⓒ Each picture of a cake represents 3 cakes.

Bakery A: 🎂 🎂 🎂 🎂 🎂 🎂 🎂 🎂

Bakery B: 🎂 🎂 🎂 🎂 🎂

Bakery C: 🎂 🎂 🎂 🎂 🎂 🎂 🎂 🎂 🎂 🎂

Bakery D: 🎂 🎂 🎂 🎂 🎂 🎂

Ⓓ Each picture of a cake represents 6 cakes.

Bakery A: 🎂 🎂 🎂 🎂

Bakery B: 🎂 🎂

Bakery C: 🎂 🎂 🎂 🎂 🎂 🎂

Bakery D: 🎂 🎂 🎂

43. The bar graph below shows the number of Math teachers, from four different states, attending a math event.

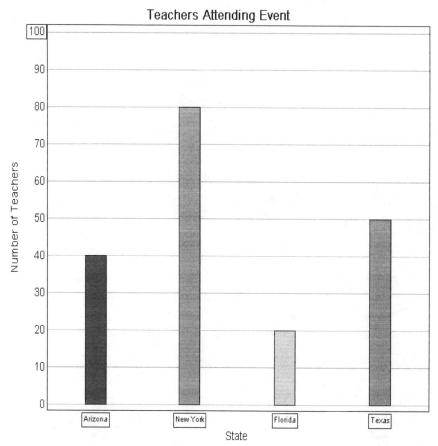

Which state has the fewest number of teachers attending the math event?

- Ⓐ Arizona
- Ⓑ New York
- Ⓒ Florida
- Ⓓ Texas

44. A student spins a spinner, with sections, labeled 1 – 8. Which of the following best represents the likelihood of the spinner landing on a 9?

- Ⓐ Likely
- Ⓑ Not likely
- Ⓒ Certain
- Ⓓ Impossible

45. A candy bowl contains 3 chocolates, 7 peppermints, and 4 lollipops. Adeline randomly draws a piece of candy from the bowl. Which of the following statements is true?

Ⓐ She is less likely to draw lollipop than a chocolate

Ⓑ She is more likely to draw a chocolate than a peppermint

Ⓒ She is more likely to draw a peppermint than a lollipop

Ⓓ She is equally likely to draw a chocolate, peppermint, or a lollipop

46. The bar graph below shows the number of votes for choosing a class mascot.

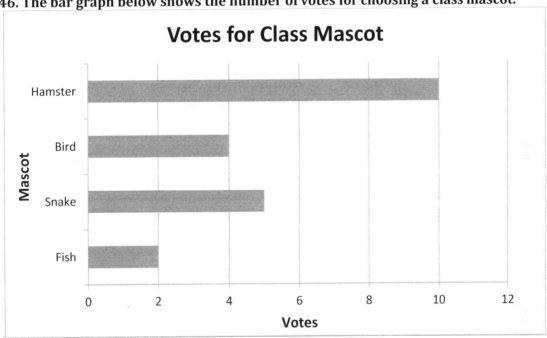

Solve and place answer on the provided griddable sheet.
How many more votes did the hamster receive than the fish?

Answers and Explanations

TEKS Standard §111.5(b)(1)(D)

1. B: The number shown for Choice B correctly shows a 2 in the hundreds place, and a 4 in the ones place.

TEKS Standard §111.5(b)(2)(D)

2. D: All numbers for Choice D have a 5 in the hundreds place, indicating that the next digit, in the tens place, must be used to make comparisons. Each digit in the tens place is different, so an examination of the ones place is not needed. The list of increasing tens place digits for Choice D are 2, 3, 4, 7, and 8, indicating a correct ordering of the numbers from least to greatest. None of the other choices show strictly increasing numbers.

TEKS Standard §111.5(b)(5)(A)

3. C: The term subtracted from means to "take away" and place a minus sign in the equation. Since 5 is being subtracted from 25, write the number 25 first followed by a minus sign and then the number 5. The problem states that this subtraction equals 5, so simply attach this to the end.

TEKS Standard §111.5(b)(3)(A)

4. D: Choice D shows 1 crayon and 3 pencils, indicating that 1 out of 4 of Camille's writing tools were crayons. The other choices are out of either a total of 7 writing tools or 5 writing tools, which cannot be used in a ratio that represents 1 out of 4.

TEKS Standard §111.5(b)(4)(A)

5. D: In order to find out the total number of hot dogs she sold in the two months, the amount sold in each month should be added. The sum of 128 and 117 is 245. Thus, she sold 245 hot dogs during the two months.

TEKS Standard §111.5(b)(4)(C)

6. D: Two dollar bills are worth $2.00. A quarter is worth $0.25, 4 dimes are worth $0.40 since they are worth $0.10 each ($4 \times 0.10 = 0.40$), 3 nickels are worth $0.15 since they are worth $0.05 each ($3 \times 0.05 = 0.15$) , and 2 pennies are worth $0.02 since each is worth $0.01. The sum of the coins is: $0.25 + $0.40 + $0.15 + $0.02, which equals $0.82. The sum of the two dollar bills and the coins can be written as: $2.00 + $0.82, which equals $2.82.

TEKS Standard §111.5(b)(4)(E)

7. D: The diagram shows 24 counters total, divided into 3 groups, with 8 counters in each group. Therefore, the total number of counters, 24, is divided by 3. This gives a quotient of 8, which is written as: $24 \div 3 = 8$.

TEKS Standard §111.5(b)(4)(G)

8. This is a simple multiplication problem which involves carrying the excess (greater than a single digit) to the next column. Start with the 9 and multiply each digit above: 9 x 8 = 72. Write down the 2 and place the 7 on top of the 7. Multiply 9 x 7 to get 63. Add in the 7 to get 70. Write down the number 70 and the product is **702**.

- 70 -

TEKS Standard §111.5(b)(4)(G)
9. B: The number of customers who entered the store can be rounded to 90. That number can be multiplied by 6, since each customer receives 6 coupons. The product of 90×6 is 540.

TEKS Standard §111.5(b)(1)(B) and (4)(A) and (4)(K)
10. A: Since a chicken has 2 feet and a horse has 4 feet, you may multiply the number of chickens found on each farm by 2, and then multiply the number of horses found on each farm by 4. After finding the total number of chicken feet and horse feet on each farm, you can then add the two amounts to find the total number of animal feet on each farm. You can then compare the two values to determine the one that is larger.

TEKS Standard §111.5(b)(3)(A)
11. B: Each model shows a whole, split into 7 sections. This makes the denominator equal to 7 for the fraction representing the shaded section for each. Since the fractions all have the same number on the bottom, the number of shaded sections can be compared. For a fraction to be more than $\frac{4}{7}$, more than 4 parts must be shaded. The model shown for Choice B shows the fraction $\frac{6}{7}$, because 6 out of 7 sections are shaded, showing a fraction that is more than 4 out of 7. The other choices all show either 4 parts or less than 4 parts shaded.

TEKS Standard §111.5(b)(2)(D)
12. B: The sequence of the number of miles walked in order from greatest to least is: 963 (Year 4), 691 (Year 1), 567 (Year 2), 221 (Year 5), 144 (Year 3). The number of miles walked can also be compared by examining only the digits in the hundreds place since they are all different. 9 is greater than 6 which is greater than 5 and so on. The only choice that shows the years for the number of miles walked in descending order is B.

TEKS Standard §111.5(b)(4)(A) and (4)(B)
13. D: $23 + 12 + 34 = 69$. Since the 9 in the ones digit is greater than or equal to five, the number is rounded up to 70.

TEKS Standard §111.5(b)(4)(C)
14. C: Convert the coins to cents and apply addition. Each nickel is worth 5 cents, so 2 nickels equals 10 cents. Each dime is worth 10 cents, so 2 dimes equals 20 cents. Each penny is worth 1 cent, so 4 pennies equals 4 cents. A quarter is worth 25 cents. $10 + 20 + 4 + 25 = 59$ cents which can be rounded to 60 cents to match one of the provided answer selections.

TEKS Standard §111.5(b)(5)
15. C: Each number is 7 more than the previous number, so adding 7 to the previous number finds the next number. Thus, the fifth number is 256, the sixth number is 263, and the seventh number is 270.

TEKS Standard §111.5(b)(4)(A) and (4)(K) and (5)
16. B: The farmer plants 17 rows of corn each season. This can be found using all of the information given in the table. The farmer had planted 34 rows of corn by the end of Season 2 and 68 rows of corn by the end of Season 4, indicating an increase of 34 rows of corn between the two seasons. So, by dividing 34 by 2, the numbers of rows planted in one season is found. Also, the farmer had planted 102 rows of corn by the end of Season 6 and

- 71 -

119 rows of corn by the end of Season 7, indicating an increase of 17 rows of corn planted in one season. If 17 rows of corn are added to the number given at the end of Season 2, the result is 51 rows of corn planted by the end of Season 3. If another 17 rows of corn are added to this amount, the farmer would have planted 68 ears of corn by the end of Season 4, which he did. Thus, he did plant 17 rows of corn each year. He had planted 136 rows of corn by the end of Season 8, 153 rows of corn by the end of Season 9, and 170 rows of corn by the end of Season 10.

TEKS Standard §111.5(b)(1)(E)

17. A: A unicycle has only one wheel; uni = one. A bicycle has two wheels; bi = two. A tricycle has three wheels; tri = three. Only answer choice A shows this correct comparison.

TEKS Standard §111.5(b)(5)(B)

18. B: A number sentence that subtracts the number of friends from the total number of stamps will not provide the number of stamps needed to give each friend. Instead, an appropriate multiplication or division number sentence within the following fact family is needed: $9 \times 5 = 45, 5 \times 9 = 45, 45 \div 9 = 5$, or $45 \div 5 = 9$.

TEKS Standard §111.5(b)(5)

19. D: The pattern displayed is an arrow pointing right, left, up, right, left....so the next arrow should be pointing up to continue the pattern.

TEKS Standard §111.5(b)(5)

20. B: The number of blocks used in each tower increases by 2. Therefore, the number of blocks used in the next four towers can be found by adding 2 to the number of blocks in the 4th tower and continuing to add 2 blocks for each tower that comes next. This gives: 10, 12, 14, and 16, with 16 blocks used in the eighth tower.

TEKS Standard §111.5(b)(5) and (4)(K)

21. D: The number of books brought by 2 students is 8, while the number of books brought by 5 students and 6 students increased by 4. Thus, the number of books brought by each student was 4. This fact can be checked by starting with 1 student and 4 books brought, and continuing the pattern to make sure it corresponds with the numbers in the table. For example, 8 students brought 32, which does in fact agree with the each student bringing 4 books. So, the number of books each student brought, 4, is multiplied by the number of students to find the total number of books that were brought. Thus, 12 students brought 12×4 books, or 48 books.

TEKS Standard §111.5(b)(6)

22. A: A vertex is a point where two or more edges meet. So, a triangular prism (Choice A) has 6 vertices, while a square pyramid (Choice B) has 5 vertices, a triangular pyramid (Choice C) has 4 vertices, and a cube (Choice D) has 8 vertices. Thus, the triangular prism is the only figure with 6 vertices.

TEKS Standard §111.5(b)(8)

23. A: Each car has 4 wheels, so the numbers of cars should be multiplied by 4 to find the total number of wheels. 3 cars will have 3×4 wheels, or 12 wheels, 4 cars will have 4×4 wheels, or 16 wheels, 7 cars will have 7×4 wheels, or 28 wheels, 11 cars will have 11×4 wheels, or 44 wheels, and 12 cars will have 12×4 wheels, or 48 wheels.

TEKS Standard §111.5(b)(6)

24. D: A line of symmetry is a line that can be drawn through a shape such that the remaining part of the shape on either side of the line looks the same, but is reflected. The shape shown is a hexagon, and it has 6 lines of symmetry. An octagon (Choice D) has 8 lines of symmetry, while an equilateral triangle (Choice A) has 3 lines of symmetry, a rhombus (Choice B) has 2 lines of symmetry, and a trapezoid (Choice C) has 1 line of symmetry. So, the only shape with more lines of symmetry than the hexagon is the octagon.

TEKS Standard §111.5(b)(3)(A)

25. C: The number line shows three marks between each whole number, making 4 equal parts between each whole number. Point S is located at $14\frac{1}{2}$ since it is halfway between 14 and 15, or 2 marks to the right of 14, which can also be written as $14\frac{2}{4}$. $14\frac{3}{4}$ is greater than that number. It is easier to see which fraction is greater if the denominators are the same, since then, just the numerators are compared. So, $14\frac{3}{4}$ is $\frac{1}{4}$ more than the number shown on the number line, and this is the only choice that is greater than the value of Point S.

TEKS Standard §111.5(b)(6)

26. B: The figure shown is a square pyramid. It indeed has 5 vertices and 5 faces. It has 8 edges, not 6 edges, so Choice B is the only statement that is not true.

TEKS Standard §111.5(b)(6)

27. C: The triangle shown for Choice C is congruent to the given triangle, since all side lengths and angles are congruent. Basically, the triangles must be the same size to be congruent, but can be flipped or rotated in any way.

TEKS Standard §111.5(b)

28. A: A triangular pyramid (Choice A) has 4 faces, while a triangular prism (Choice B) and a rectangular pyramid (Choice D) both have 5 faces. A cube (Choice C) has 6 faces. Thus, the only figure with less than 5 faces is the triangular pyramid.

TEKS Standard §111.5(b)(6)(A)

29. D: Figures A, B, and C can all be folded in a manner that the squares lay directly on top of each other. This cannot be done with Figure D; therefore, Figure D does not have a line of symmetry.

TEKS Standard §111.5(b)(6)(A)

30. C: A circle is a two-dimensional shape that is not a polygon. It does not have straight sides that meet at vertices. All of the other choices are two-dimensional polygons.

TEKS Standard §111.5(b)(6)(A)

31. D: The shapes all have at least 6 edges, with a triangular pyramid having 6 edges, a triangular prism having 9 edges, and a square pyramid having 8 edges. These shapes are clearly not all pyramids or all prisms, and they do not all have 5 faces (the triangular prism and square pyramid both have 5 faces but the triangular pyramid has only 4 faces). So, Choice D is the only statement common to all of the shapes.

- 73 -

TEKS Standard §111.5(b)(7)(B)

32. B: The perimeter is the sum of the lengths of all five sides, or $5 + 5 + 3 + 3 + 4$, which equals 20. Therefore, the perimeter of the pentagon is 20 cm.

TEKS Standard §111.5(b)(7)(B)

33. B: To find the perimeter of each shape, add up the lengths of all of the sides. The square has four sides of equal length, so it has a perimeter of 16 centimeters, which is larger than the perimeters of the other three shapes. The triangle and rectangle each have a perimeter of 14 centimeters. The hexagon has a perimeter of 12 centimeters.

TEKS Standard §111.5(b)(7)

34. B: The pencil is approximately 3.25 inches, which rounds to 3 inches.

TEKS Standard §111.5(b)(7)

35. C: The width of the notebook can be estimated by marking off lengths that are close to the measurement of a centimeter. The width of the book is slightly less than 5.5 cm, so it is about 5 cm.

TEKS Standard §111.5(b)(6)(D)

36. D: The triangle includes 21 whole square units, plus 7 one-half square units, or $3\frac{1}{2}$ square units. So, 21 square units plus $3\frac{1}{2}$ square units gives a total of $24\frac{1}{2}$ square units.

TEKS Standard §111.5(b)(7)(B)

37. The perimeter of a figure is the sum of all of its sides. Since a rectangle's width and length will be the same on opposite sides, the perimeter of a rectangle can be calculated by using the following formula: perimeter = 2 x width + 2 x length
Using the numbers given in the question:
perimeter = 2 x 7cm + 2 x 9cm)
perimeter = 14cm + 18cm
perimeter = **32cm**

TEKS Standard §111.5(b)(7)

38. D: The thermometer shows 4 marks between each whole number, or 5 intervals. This means each interval on the thermometer represents 2 degrees since there are 5 intervals between each difference of 10 degrees. The thermometer reveals a reading at 4 degrees above 70 degrees (2 marks above 70), or 6 degrees below 80 degrees (3 marks below 80). Thus, the temperature outside is 74 degrees Fahrenheit.

TEKS Standard §111.5(b)(7)

39. A: The short hand, or hour hand, is between 10 o'clock and 11 o'clock, revealing that Amanda arrived after 10 o'clock, but before 11 o'clock. It is much closer to the 10, so this indicates the time is much closer to 10 o'clock than 11 o'clock. The long hand, or minute hand, is pointing to the 2, indicating 10 minutes after the hour. This is because for minutes, each number represents 5 minutes; so $2 \times 5 = 10$. So, she arrived at the party at 10:10.

TEKS Standard §111.5(b)(7)

40. B: Since there are sixty minutes in an hour, a "quarter" in time represents 15 minutes. A quarter past three would mean 15 minutes after 3 o'clock or 3:15. Represented on an analog clock, the big hand would be pointing to the three and the small hand pointing just past the three.

TEKS Standard §111.5(b)(8)

41. B: There are 6 yellow cards and 3 red cards. The more cards there are of a certain color, the more likely it is that the color is drawn. With more yellow cards than red cards in the bag, he is more likely to draw a yellow card than a red card. There are more green cards than yellow cards, so he is more likely to draw a green card than a yellow card. There are less yellow cards than blue cards, so he is less likely to draw a yellow card than a blue card. Finally, the number of red, blue, green, and yellow cards are all different – so none of them are equally likely to be drawn compared to another color. Thus, Choice B is the only true statement.

TEKS Standard §111,5(b)(8)

42. A: The pictograph for Choice A reveals that each picture of a cake represents 5 actual cakes. Therefore, the numbers given in the table, divided by 5, should equal the number of cakes represented in the pictograph. The pictograph accurately shows 5 cakes for 25 actual cakes, 3 cakes for 15 actual cakes, 7 cakes for 35 actual cakes, and 4 cakes for 20 actual cakes. This is the only pictograph that represents the correct number of cakes.

TEKS Standard §111.5(b)(8)

43. C: Florida had 20 teachers that attended the event, which is less than the number of teachers who attended the event from each of the other three states. The number of teachers that attended the event from each of the other states were 40 (Arizona), 80 (New York), and 50 (California). Also, just looking at the bar graph shows that Florida had the least number of teachers attend compared to the other states because the bar is much lower in the graph.

TEKS Standard §111.5(b)(8)

44. D: Since the spinner only has sections, labeled 1 – 8, there is not a section, labeled "9". Therefore, it is impossible for the spinner to land on a 9.

TEKS Standard §111.5(b)(8)

45. C: The more candy there is of a certain kind, the more likely it is that the candy is drawn. With more lollipops than chocolates in the bowl, she is more likely to draw a lollipop than a chocolate. There are more peppermints than chocolates, so she is more likely to draw a peppermint than a chocolate. There are more peppermints than lollipops, so she is more likely to draw a peppermint than a lollipop. Finally, the number of chocolates, peppermints, and lollipops are all different – so none of them are equally likely to be drawn compared to another color. Thus, Choice C is the only true statement.

TEKS Standard §111.5(b)(8)

46. The hamster received 10 votes and the fish received 2 votes. The difference is 10 – 2 = **8 votes**.

General Strategies

The most important thing you can do is to ignore your fears and jump into the test immediately- do not be overwhelmed by any strange-sounding terms. You have to jump into the test like jumping into a pool- all at once is the easiest way.

Make Predictions

As you read and understand the question, try to guess what the answer will be. Remember that several of the answer choices are wrong, and once you begin reading them, your mind will immediately become cluttered with answer choices designed to throw you off. Your mind is typically the most focused immediately after you have read the question and digested its contents. If you can, try to predict what the correct answer will be. You may be surprised at what you can predict.

Quickly scan the choices and see if your prediction is in the listed answer choices. If it is, then you can be quite confident that you have the right answer. It still won't hurt to check the other answer choices, but most of the time, you've got it!

Answer the Question

It may seem obvious to only pick answer choices that answer the question, but the test writers can create some excellent answer choices that are wrong. Don't pick an answer just because it sounds right, or you believe it to be true. It MUST answer the question. Once you've made your selection, always go back and check it against the question and make sure that you didn't misread the question, and the answer choice does answer the question posed.

Benchmark

After you read the first answer choice, decide if you think it sounds correct or not. If it doesn't, move on to the next answer choice. If it does, mentally mark that answer choice. This doesn't mean that you've definitely selected it as your answer choice, it just means that it's the best you've seen thus far. Go ahead and read the next choice. If the next choice is worse than the one you've already selected, keep going to the next answer choice. If the next choice is better than the choice you've already selected, mentally mark the new answer choice as your best guess.

The first answer choice that you select becomes your standard. Every other answer choice must be benchmarked against that standard. That choice is correct until proven otherwise by another answer choice beating it out. Once you've decided that no other answer choice seems as good, do one final check to ensure that your answer choice answers the question posed.

Valid Information

Don't discount any of the information provided in the question. Every piece of information may be necessary to determine the correct answer. None of the information in the question is there to throw you off (while the answer choices will certainly have information to throw you off). If two seemingly unrelated topics are discussed, don't ignore either. You can be confident there is a relationship, or it wouldn't be included in the question, and you are probably going to have to determine what is that relationship to find the answer.

Avoid "Fact Traps"

Don't get distracted by a choice that is factually true. Your search is for the answer that answers the question. Stay focused and don't fall for an answer that is true but incorrect. Always go back to the question and make sure you're choosing an answer that actually answers the question and is not just a true statement. An answer can be factually correct, but it MUST answer the question asked. Additionally, two answers can both be seemingly correct, so be sure to read all of the answer choices, and make sure that you get the one that BEST answers the question.

Milk the Question

Some of the questions may throw you completely off. They might deal with a subject you have not been exposed to, or one that you haven't reviewed in years. While your lack of knowledge about the subject will be a hindrance, the question itself can give you many clues that will help you find the correct answer. Read the question carefully and look for clues. Watch particularly for adjectives and nouns describing difficult terms or words that you don't recognize. Regardless of if you completely understand a word or not, replacing it with a synonym either provided or one you more familiar with may help you to understand what the questions are asking. Rather than wracking your mind about specific detailed information concerning a difficult term or word, try to use mental substitutes that are easier to understand.

The Trap of Familiarity

Don't just choose a word because you recognize it. On difficult questions, you may not recognize a number of words in the answer choices. The test writers don't put "make-believe" words on the test; so don't think that just because you only recognize all the words in one answer choice means that answer choice must be correct. If you only recognize words in one answer choice, then focus on that one. Is it correct? Try your best to determine if it is correct. If it is, that is great, but if it doesn't, eliminate it. Each word and answer choice you eliminate increases your chances of getting the question correct, even if you then have to guess among the unfamiliar choices.

Eliminate Answers

Eliminate choices as soon as you realize they are wrong. But be careful! Make sure you consider all of the possible answer choices. Just because one appears right, doesn't mean that the next one won't be even better! The test writers will usually put more than one good answer choice for every question, so read all of them. Don't worry if you are stuck between two that seem right. By getting down to just two remaining possible choices, your odds are now 50/50. Rather than wasting too much time, play the odds. You are guessing, but guessing wisely, because you've been able to knock out some of the answer choices that you know are wrong. If you are eliminating choices and realize that the last answer choice you are left with is also obviously wrong, don't panic. Start over and consider each choice again. There may easily be something that you missed the first time and will realize on the second pass.

Tough Questions

If you are stumped on a problem or it appears too hard or too difficult, don't waste time. Move on! Remember though, if you can quickly check for obviously incorrect answer choices, your chances of guessing correctly are greatly improved. Before you completely give up, at least try to knock out a couple of possible answers. Eliminate what you can and then guess at the remaining answer choices before moving on.

Brainstorm

If you get stuck on a difficult question, spend a few seconds quickly brainstorming. Run through the complete list of possible answer choices. Look at each choice and ask yourself, "Could this answer the question satisfactorily?" Go through each answer choice and consider it independently of the other. By systematically going through all possibilities, you may find something that you would otherwise overlook. Remember that when you get stuck, it's important to try to keep moving.

Read Carefully

Understand the problem. Read the question and answer choices carefully. Don't miss the question because you misread the terms. You have plenty of time to read each question thoroughly and make sure you understand what is being asked. Yet a happy medium must be attained, so don't waste too much time. You must read carefully, but efficiently.

Face Value

When in doubt, use common sense. Always accept the situation in the problem at face value. Don't read too much into it. These problems will not require you to make huge leaps of logic. The test writers aren't trying to throw you off with a cheap trick. If you have to go beyond creativity and make a leap of logic in order to have an answer choice answer the question, then you should look at the other answer choices. Don't overcomplicate the problem by creating theoretical relationships or explanations that will warp time or space. These are normal problems rooted in reality. It's just that the applicable relationship or explanation may not be readily apparent and you have to figure things out. Use your common sense to interpret anything that isn't clear.

Prefixes

If you're having trouble with a word in the question or answer choices, try dissecting it. Take advantage of every clue that the word might include. Prefixes and suffixes can be a huge help. Usually they allow you to determine a basic meaning. Pre- means before, post- means after, pro - is positive, de- is negative. From these prefixes and suffixes, you can get an idea of the general meaning of the word and try to put it into context. Beware though of any traps. Just because con is the opposite of pro, doesn't necessarily mean congress is the opposite of progress!

Hedge Phrases

Watch out for critical "hedge" phrases, such as likely, may, can, will often, sometimes, often, almost, mostly, usually, generally, rarely, sometimes. Question writers insert these hedge phrases to cover every possibility. Often an answer choice will be wrong simply because it leaves no room for exception. Avoid answer choices that have definitive words like "exactly," and "always".

Switchback Words

Stay alert for "switchbacks". These are the words and phrases frequently used to alert you to shifts in thought. The most common switchback word is "but". Others include although, however, nevertheless, on the other hand, even though, while, in spite of, despite, regardless of.

New Information

Correct answer choices will rarely have completely new information included. Answer choices typically are straightforward reflections of the material asked about and will directly relate to the question. If a new piece of information is included in an answer choice that doesn't even seem to relate to the topic being asked about, then that answer choice is likely incorrect. All of the information needed to answer the question is usually provided for you, and so you should not have to make guesses that are unsupported or choose answer choices that require unknown information that cannot be reasoned on its own.

Time Management

On technical questions, don't get lost on the technical terms. Don't spend too much time on any one question. If you don't know what a term means, then since you don't have a dictionary, odds are you aren't going to get much further. You should immediately recognize terms as whether or not you know them. If you don't, work with the other clues that you have, the other answer choices and terms provided, but don't waste too much time trying to figure out a difficult term.

Contextual Clues

Look for contextual clues. An answer can be right but not correct. The contextual clues will help you find the answer that is most right and is correct. Understand the context in which a phrase or statement is made. This will help you make important distinctions.

Don't Panic

Panicking will not answer any questions for you. Therefore, it isn't helpful. When you first see the question, if your mind goes blank, take a deep breath. Force yourself to mechanically go through the steps of solving the problem and using the strategies you've learned.

Pace Yourself

Don't get clock fever. It's easy to be overwhelmed when you're looking at a page full of questions, your mind is full of random thoughts and feeling confused, and the clock is ticking down faster than you would like. Calm down and maintain the pace that you have set for yourself. As long as you are on track by monitoring your pace, you are guaranteed to have enough time for yourself. When you get to the last few minutes of the test, it may seem like you won't have enough time left, but if you only have as many questions as you should have left at that point, then you're right on track!

Answer Selection

The best way to pick an answer choice is to eliminate all of those that are wrong, until only one is left and confirm that is the correct answer. Sometimes though, an answer choice may immediately look right. Be careful! Take a second to make sure that the other choices are not equally obvious. Don't make a hasty mistake. There are only two times that you should stop before checking other answers. First is when you are positive that the answer choice you have selected is correct. Second is when time is almost out and you have to make a quick guess!

Check Your Work

Since you will probably not know every term listed and the answer to every question, it is important that you get credit for the ones that you do know. Don't miss any questions through careless mistakes. If at all possible, try to take a second to look back over your answer selection and make sure you've selected the correct answer choice and haven't made a costly careless mistake (such as marking an answer choice that you didn't mean to mark). This quick double check should more than pay for itself in caught mistakes for the time it costs.

Beware of Directly Quoted Answers

Sometimes an answer choice will repeat word for word a portion of the question or reference section. However, beware of such exact duplication – it may be a trap! More than likely, the correct choice will paraphrase or summarize a point, rather than being exactly the same wording.

Slang

Scientific sounding answers are better than slang ones. An answer choice that begins "To compare the outcomes..." is much more likely to be correct than one that begins "Because some people insisted..."

Extreme Statements

Avoid wild answers that throw out highly controversial ideas that are proclaimed as established fact. An answer choice that states the "process should be used in certain situations, if..." is much more likely to be correct than one that states the "process should be discontinued completely." The first is a calm rational statement and doesn't even make a definitive, uncompromising stance, using a hedge word "if" to provide wiggle room, whereas the second choice is a radical idea and far more extreme.

Answer Choice Families

When you have two or more answer choices that are direct opposites or parallels, one of them is usually the correct answer. For instance, if one answer choice states "x increases" and another answer choice states "x decreases" or "y increases," then those two or three answer choices are very similar in construction and fall into the same family of answer choices. A family of answer choices is when two or three answer choices are very similar in construction, and yet often have a directly opposite meaning. Usually the correct answer choice will be in that family of answer choices. The "odd man out" or answer choice that doesn't seem to fit the parallel construction of the other answer choices is more likely to be incorrect.

How to Overcome Test Anxiety

The very nature of tests caters to some level of anxiety, nervousness or tension, just as we feel for any important event that occurs in our lives. A little bit of anxiety or nervousness can be a good thing. It helps us with motivation, and makes achievement just that much sweeter. However, too much anxiety can be a problem; especially if it hinders our ability to function and perform.

"Test anxiety," is the term that refers to the emotional reactions that some test-takers experience when faced with a test or exam. Having a fear of testing and exams is based upon a rational fear, since the test-taker's performance can shape the course of an academic career. Nevertheless, experiencing excessive fear of examinations will only interfere with the test-takers ability to perform, and his/her chances to be successful.

There are a large variety of causes that can contribute to the development and sensation of test anxiety. These include, but are not limited to lack of performance and worrying about issues surrounding the test.

Lack of Preparation

Lack of preparation can be identified by the following behaviors or situations:

Not scheduling enough time to study, and therefore cramming the night before the test or exam
Managing time poorly, to create the sensation that there is not enough time to do everything
Failing to organize the text information in advance, so that the study material consists of the entire text and not simply the pertinent information
Poor overall studying habits

Worrying, on the other hand, can be related to both the test taker, or many other factors around him/her that will be affected by the results of the test. These include worrying about:

Previous performances on similar exams, or exams in general
How friends and other students are achieving
The negative consequences that will result from a poor grade or failure

There are three primary elements to test anxiety. Physical components, which involve the same typical bodily reactions as those to acute anxiety (to be discussed below). Emotional factors have to do with fear or panic. Mental or cognitive issues concerning attention spans and memory abilities.

Physical Signals

There are many different symptoms of test anxiety, and these are not limited to mental and emotional strain. Frequently there are a range of physical signals that will let a test taker know that he/she is suffering from test anxiety. These bodily changes can include the following:

Perspiring
Sweaty palms
Wet, trembling hands
Nausea
Dry mouth
A knot in the stomach
Headache
Faintness
Muscle tension
Aching shoulders, back and neck
Rapid heart beat
Feeling too hot/cold

To recognize the sensation of test anxiety, a test-taker should monitor him/herself for the following sensations:

The physical distress symptoms as listed above
Emotional sensitivity, expressing emotional feelings such as the need to cry or laugh too much, or a sensation of anger or helplessness
A decreased ability to think, causing the test-taker to blank out or have racing thoughts that are hard to organize or control.

Though most students will feel some level of anxiety when faced with a test or exam, the majority can cope with that anxiety and maintain it at a manageable level. However, those who cannot are faced with a very real and very serious condition, which can and should be controlled for the immeasurable benefit of this sufferer.

Naturally, these sensations lead to negative results for the testing experience. The most common effects of test anxiety have to do with nervousness and mental blocking.

Nervousness

Nervousness can appear in several different levels:

The test-taker's difficulty, or even inability to read and understand the questions on the test
The difficulty or inability to organize thoughts to a coherent form
The difficulty or inability to recall key words and concepts relating to the testing questions (especially essays)
The receipt of poor grades on a test, though the test material was well known by the test taker

Conversely, a person may also experience mental blocking, which involves:

Blanking out on test questions
Only remembering the correct answers to the questions when the test has already finished.

Fortunately for test anxiety sufferers, beating these feelings, to a large degree, has to do with proper preparation. When a test taker has a feeling of preparedness, then anxiety will be dramatically lessened.

The first step to resolving anxiety issues is to distinguish which of the two types of anxiety are being suffered. If the anxiety is a direct result of a lack of preparation, this should be considered a normal reaction, and the anxiety level (as opposed to the test results) shouldn't be anything to worry about. However, if, when adequately prepared, the test-taker still panics, blanks out, or seems to overreact, this is not a fully rational reaction. While this can be considered normal too, there are many ways to combat and overcome these effects.

Remember that anxiety cannot be entirely eliminated, however, there are ways to minimize it, to make the anxiety easier to manage. Preparation is one of the best ways to minimize test anxiety. Therefore the following techniques are wise in order to best fight off any anxiety that may want to build.

To begin with, try to avoid cramming before a test, whenever it is possible. By trying to memorize an entire term's worth of information in one day, you'll be shocking your system, and not giving yourself a very good chance to absorb the information. This is an easy path to anxiety, so for those who suffer from test anxiety, cramming should not even be considered an option.

Instead of cramming, work throughout the semester to combine all of the material which is presented throughout the semester, and work on it gradually as the course goes by, making sure to master the main concepts first, leaving minor details for a week or so before the test.

To study for the upcoming exam, be sure to pose questions that may be on the examination, to gauge the ability to answer them by integrating the ideas from your texts, notes and lectures, as well as any supplementary readings.

If it is truly impossible to cover all of the information that was covered in that particular term, concentrate on the most important portions, that can be covered very well. Learn these concepts as best as possible, so that when the test comes, a goal can be made to use these concepts as presentations of your knowledge.

In addition to study habits, changes in attitude are critical to beating a struggle with test anxiety. In fact, an improvement of the perspective over the entire test-taking experience can actually help a test taker to enjoy studying and therefore improve the overall experience. Be certain not to overemphasize the significance of the grade - know that the result of the test is neither a reflection of self worth, nor is it a measure of intelligence; one grade will not predict a person's future success.

To improve an overall testing outlook, the following steps should be tried:

Keeping in mind that the most reasonable expectation for taking a test is to expect to try to demonstrate as much of what you know as you possibly can.
Reminding ourselves that a test is only one test; this is not the only one, and there will be others.
The thought of thinking of oneself in an irrational, all-or-nothing term should be avoided at all costs.
A reward should be designated for after the test, so there's something to look forward to. Whether it be going to a movie, going out to eat, or simply visiting friends, schedule it in advance, and do it no matter what result is expected on the exam.

Test-takers should also keep in mind that the basics are some of the most important things, even beyond anti-anxiety techniques and studying. Never neglect the basic social, emotional and biological needs, in order to try to absorb information. In order to best achieve, these three factors must be held as just as important as the studying itself.

Study Steps

Remember the following important steps for studying:

Maintain healthy nutrition and exercise habits. Continue both your recreational activities and social pass times. These both contribute to your physical and emotional well being.
Be certain to get a good amount of sleep, especially the night before the test, because when you're overtired you are not able to perform to the best of your best ability.
Keep the studying pace to a moderate level by taking breaks when they are needed, and varying the work whenever possible, to keep the mind fresh instead of getting bored. When enough studying has been done that all the material that can be learned has been learned, and the test taker is prepared for the test, stop studying and do something relaxing such as listening to music, watching a movie, or taking a warm bubble bath.

There are also many other techniques to minimize the uneasiness or apprehension that is experienced along with test anxiety before, during, or even after the examination. In fact, there are a great deal of things that can be done to stop anxiety from interfering with lifestyle and performance. Again, remember that anxiety will not be eliminated entirely, and it shouldn't be. Otherwise that "up" feeling for exams would not exist, and most of us depend on that sensation to perform better than usual. However, this anxiety has to be at a level that is manageable.

Of course, as we have just discussed, being prepared for the exam is half the battle right away. Attending all classes, finding out what knowledge will be expected on the exam, and knowing the exam schedules are easy steps to lowering anxiety. Keeping up with work will remove the need to cram, and efficient study habits will eliminate wasted time. Studying should be done in an ideal location for concentration, so that it is simple to become interested in the material and give it complete attention. A method such as SQ3R (Survey, Question, Read, Recite, Review) is a wonderful key to follow to make sure that the study habits are as effective as possible, especially in the case of learning from a textbook. Flashcards are great techniques for memorization. Learning to take good

- 84 -

notes will mean that notes will be full of useful information, so that less sifting will need to be done to seek out what is pertinent for studying. Reviewing notes after class and then again on occasion will keep the information fresh in the mind. From notes that have been taken summary sheets and outlines can be made for simpler reviewing.

A study group can also be a very motivational and helpful place to study, as there will be a sharing of ideas, all of the minds can work together, to make sure that everyone understands, and the studying will be made more interesting because it will be a social occasion.

Basically, though, as long as the test-taker remains organized and self confident, with efficient study habits, less time will need to be spent studying, and higher grades will be achieved.

To become self confident, there are many useful steps. The first of these is "self talk." It has been shown through extensive research, that self-talk for students who suffer from test anxiety, should be well monitored, in order to make sure that it contributes to self confidence as opposed to sinking the student. Frequently the self talk of test-anxious students is negative or self-defeating, thinking that everyone else is smarter and faster, that they always mess up, and that if they don't do well, they'll fail the entire course. It is important to decreasing anxiety that awareness is made of self talk. Try writing any negative self thoughts and then disputing them with a positive statement instead. Begin self-encouragement as though it was a friend speaking. Repeat positive statements to help reprogram the mind to believing in successes instead of failures.

Helpful Techniques

Other extremely helpful techniques include:

Self-visualization of doing well and reaching goals
While aiming for an "A" level of understanding, don't try to "overprotect" by setting your expectations lower. This will only convince the mind to stop studying in order to meet the lower expectations.
Don't make comparisons with the results or habits of other students. These are individual factors, and different things work for different people, causing different results.
Strive to become an expert in learning what works well, and what can be done in order to improve. Consider collecting this data in a journal.
Create rewards for after studying instead of doing things before studying that will only turn into avoidance behaviors.
Make a practice of relaxing - by using methods such as progressive relaxation, self-hypnosis, guided imagery, etc - in order to make relaxation an automatic sensation.
Work on creating a state of relaxed concentration so that concentrating will take on the focus of the mind, so that none will be wasted on worrying.
Take good care of the physical self by eating well and getting enough sleep.
Plan in time for exercise and stick to this plan.

Beyond these techniques, there are other methods to be used before, during and after the test that will help the test-taker perform well in addition to overcoming anxiety.

Before the exam comes the academic preparation. This involves establishing a study schedule and beginning at least one week before the actual date of the test. By doing this, the anxiety of not having enough time to study for the test will be automatically eliminated. Moreover, this will make the studying a much more effective experience, ensuring that the learning will be an easier process. This relieves much undue pressure on the test-taker.

Summary sheets, note cards, and flash cards with the main concepts and examples of these main concepts should be prepared in advance of the actual studying time. A topic should never be eliminated from this process. By omitting a topic because it isn't expected to be on the test is only setting up the test-taker for anxiety should it actually appear on the exam. Utilize the course syllabus for laying out the topics that should be studied. Carefully go over the notes that were made in class, paying special attention to any of the issues that the professor took special care to emphasize while lecturing in class. In the textbooks, use the chapter review, or if possible, the chapter tests, to begin your review.

It may even be possible to ask the instructor what information will be covered on the exam, or what the format of the exam will be (for example, multiple choice, essay, free form, true-false). Additionally, see if it is possible to find out how many questions will be on the test. If a review sheet or sample test has been offered by the professor, make good use of it, above anything else, for the preparation for the test. Another great resource for getting to know the examination is reviewing tests from previous semesters. Use these tests to review, and aim to achieve a 100% score on each of the possible topics. With a few exceptions, the goal that you set for yourself is the highest one that you will reach.

Take all of the questions that were assigned as homework, and rework them to any other possible course material. The more problems reworked, the more skill and confidence will form as a result. When forming the solution to a problem, write out each of the steps. Don't simply do head work. By doing as many steps on paper as possible, much clarification and therefore confidence will be formed. Do this with as many homework problems as possible, before checking the answers. By checking the answer after each problem, a reinforcement will exist, that will not be on the exam. Study situations should be as exam-like as possible, to prime the test-taker's system for the experience. By waiting to check the answers at the end, a psychological advantage will be formed, to decrease the stress factor.

Another fantastic reason for not cramming is the avoidance of confusion in concepts, especially when it comes to mathematics. 8-10 hours of study will become one hundred percent more effective if it is spread out over a week or at least several days, instead of doing it all in one sitting. Recognize that the human brain requires time in order to assimilate new material, so frequent breaks and a span of study time over several days will be much more beneficial.

Additionally, don't study right up until the point of the exam. Studying should stop a minimum of one hour before the exam begins. This allows the brain to rest and put things in their proper order. This will also provide the time to become as relaxed as possible when going into the examination room. The test-taker will also have time to eat well and eat sensibly. Know that the brain needs food as much as the rest of the body. With enough food and enough sleep, as well as a relaxed attitude, the body and the mind are primed for success.

Avoid any anxious classmates who are talking about the exam. These students only spread anxiety, and are not worth sharing the anxious sentimentalities.

Before the test also involves creating a positive attitude, so mental preparation should also be a point of concentration. There are many keys to creating a positive attitude. Should fears become rushing in, make a visualization of taking the exam, doing well, and seeing an A written on the paper. Write out a list of affirmations that will bring a feeling of confidence, such as "I am doing well in my English class," "I studied well and know my material," "I enjoy this class." Even if the affirmations aren't believed at first, it sends a positive message to the subconscious which will result in an alteration of the overall belief system, which is the system that creates reality.

If a sensation of panic begins, work with the fear and imagine the very worst! Work through the entire scenario of not passing the test, failing the entire course, and dropping out of school, followed by not getting a job, and pushing a shopping cart through the dark alley where you'll live. This will place things into perspective! Then, practice deep breathing and create a visualization of the opposite situation - achieving an "A" on the exam, passing the entire course, receiving the degree at a graduation ceremony.

On the day of the test, there are many things to be done to ensure the best results, as well as the most calm outlook. The following stages are suggested in order to maximize test-taking potential:

Begin the examination day with a moderate breakfast, and avoid any coffee or beverages with caffeine if the test taker is prone to jitters. Even people who are used to managing caffeine can feel jittery or light-headed when it is taken on a test day. Attempt to do something that is relaxing before the examination begins. As last minute cramming clouds the mastering of overall concepts, it is better to use this time to create a calming outlook.
Be certain to arrive at the test location well in advance, in order to provide time to select a location that is away from doors, windows and other distractions, as well as giving enough time to relax before the test begins.
Keep away from anxiety generating classmates who will upset the sensation of stability and relaxation that is being attempted before the exam.
Should the waiting period before the exam begins cause anxiety, create a self-distraction by reading a light magazine or something else that is relaxing and simple.

During the exam itself, read the entire exam from beginning to end, and find out how much time should be allotted to each individual problem. Once writing the exam, should more time be taken for a problem, it should be abandoned, in order to begin another problem. If there is time at the end, the unfinished problem can always be returned to and completed.

Read the instructions very carefully - twice - so that unpleasant surprises won't follow during or after the exam has ended.

When writing the exam, pretend that the situation is actually simply the completion of homework within a library, or at home. This will assist in forming a relaxed atmosphere, and will allow the brain extra focus for the complex thinking function.

Begin the exam with all of the questions with which the most confidence is felt. This will build the confidence level regarding the entire exam and will begin a quality momentum. This will also create encouragement for trying the problems where uncertainty resides.

Going with the "gut instinct" is always the way to go when solving a problem. Second guessing should be avoided at all costs. Have confidence in the ability to do well.

For essay questions, create an outline in advance that will keep the mind organized and make certain that all of the points are remembered. For multiple choice, read every answer, even if the correct one has been spotted - a better one may exist.

Continue at a pace that is reasonable and not rushed, in order to be able to work carefully. Provide enough time to go over the answers at the end, to check for small errors that can be corrected.

Should a feeling of panic begin, breathe deeply, and think of the feeling of the body releasing sand through its pores. Visualize a calm, peaceful place, and include all of the sights, sounds and sensations of this image. Continue the deep breathing, and take a few minutes to continue this with closed eyes. When all is well again, return to the test.

If a "blanking" occurs for a certain question, skip it and move on to the next question. There will be time to return to the other question later. Get everything done that can be done, first, to guarantee all the grades that can be compiled, and to build all of the confidence possible. Then return to the weaker questions to build the marks from there.

Remember, one's own reality can be created, so as long as the belief is there, success will follow. And remember: anxiety can happen later, right now, there's an exam to be written!

After the examination is complete, whether there is a feeling for a good grade or a bad grade, don't dwell on the exam, and be certain to follow through on the reward that was promised...and enjoy it! Don't dwell on any mistakes that have been made, as there is nothing that can be done at this point anyway.

Additionally, don't begin to study for the next test right away. Do something relaxing for a while, and let the mind relax and prepare itself to begin absorbing information again.

From the results of the exam - both the grade and the entire experience, be certain to learn from what has gone on. Perfect studying habits and work some more on confidence in order to make the next examination experience even better than the last one.

Learn to avoid places where openings occurred for laziness, procrastination and day dreaming.

Use the time between this exam and the next one to better learn to relax, even learning to relax on cue, so that any anxiety can be controlled during the next exam. Learn how to relax the body. Slouch in your chair if that helps. Tighten and then relax all of the different muscle groups, one group at a time, beginning with the feet and then working all the way up to the neck and face. This will ultimately relax the muscles more than they were to begin with. Learn how to breathe deeply and comfortably, and focus on this breathing going in and out as a relaxing thought. With every exhale, repeat the word "relax."

As common as test anxiety is, it is very possible to overcome it. Make yourself one of the test-takers who overcome this frustrating hindrance.

Additional Bonus Material

Due to our efforts to try to keep this book to a manageable length, we've created a link that will give you access to all of your additional bonus material.

Please visit http://www.mometrix.com/bonus948/staarg3math to access the information.